HOME, AND HOME AGAIN

By George and Helen Papashvily

HOME, AND HOME AGAIN

THANKS TO NOAH

YES AND NO STORIES

ANYTHING CAN HAPPEN

By Helen Papashvily

ALL THE HAPPY ENDINGS

NEW YORK, EVANSTON, SAN FRANCISCO, LONDON

HOME,
AND HOME
AGAIN

George and Helen Papashvily

HARPER & ROW, PUBLISHERS

HOME, AND HOME AGAIN. Copyright © 1973 by George and Helen Waite Papashvily. All rights reserved. Printed in the United States of America. No part of this book may be used or reproduced in any manner whatsoever without written permission except in the case of brief quotations embodied in critical articles and reviews. For information address Harper & Row, Publishers, Inc., 10 East 53rd Street, New York, N.Y. 10022. Published simultaneously in Canada by Fitzhenry & Whiteside Limited, Toronto.

FIRST EDITION

Designed by Sidney Feinberg

Library of Congress Cataloging in Publication Data

Papashvily, George.
    Home, and Home Again.
    1. Papashvily, George.   2. Georgia (Transcaucosia)
—Description and travel.   I. Papashvily, Helen
(Waite), joint author.   II. Title.
E169.5.P3A34   1973   914.7'95'04840924   [B]
ISBN 0–06–013262–0   73–4114

For
Ruth Adams
and
Dorothy Boyer
and
Charles and Wilma Muhlenberg,
who made the journey possible.

HOME, AND HOME AGAIN

*N*ow the airplane takes off, and at last, after forty years, I am going home. From the day I left my village in the Caucasus I waited for this moment.

In Persia, in Turkey, and then in the United States, wandering from place to place, living in dark rooms, lost in the crowded streets, working at a hundred jobs, a stranger in a strange land, I cheered myself through the loneliest hours thinking how one day I would go back to Georgia; I would walk up the mountainside where my foot knew every stone; I would see my father's face again; I would eat the bread and drink the wine of home.

When I met and married an American girl, the first promise I made her was that I would take her to Georgia. But there came the Depression and then the war, and in those long years I built a new life. I was an American citizen. I had a home. I had work. At first I was a farmer, then a mechanic, and finally a sculptor. My days were full of the present.

Time went by. The few letters I received told me little. During the war and for two years afterward I heard nothing at all. When at last word came it was to say my father and my aunt were dead. After that I did not think of Georgia so often. And yet—I did not forget.

Spring never came to our Pennsylvania hillsides but I remembered the Cornelian cherries would be in golden bloom above Dushet, and when it was harvest time, I always wondered who gathers now the grapes my aunt planted, who sits in the dappled sun beneath her arbor, who drinks the wine? When I dreamed, I dreamed always of Kobiantkari where I was born, a village on the mountainside above a stream that has no name but "Our Own."

How often I thought to return, but somehow it was never possible. Time and money, as everybody knows, seldom keep company and where one is the other is not, and so it was with me. But finally a day came when by chance I had both, and I said to my wife, "Let us go to Georgia."

"When?"

"As soon as we can pack our suitcases."

Except I discovered it was not that easy.

One has first to be photographed and registered and documented and stuck full of needles and go to farewell parties and apply for visas and between times listen to the travel agent who wanted to sell a few bargains in other countries he had on hand.

Over and over I explained to him I don't want the French

châteaux country, Italian hill towns, or Ceylon, or Honolulu with a complimentary luau, no, and not Holland with every tulip in bloom. My village, Kobiantkari, is enough.

"Ah, yes, but I must remind you," the travel agent said, "that your visa permits you to go only to Tbilisi, which is, I believe, the capital city, and the immediate area around it."

"How immediate?"

"According to regulations, within thirty miles."

"But my village is thirty-four miles from Tbilisi. I covered every foot of the ground between Kobiantkari and Tbilisi hundreds of times—driving turkeys or sheep, going to market, just taking myself for a walk, and I know exactly where thirty miles brings me—to the turn of the road at the top of a mountain where you can, if the day is clear, first see the smoke of our fires."

"That is most unfortunate," the travel agent said, "but Russian nationals in the United States are restricted to certain areas, and the same applies to Americans in the Soviet Union."

I never heard of anything so foolish in my life. Does anybody think a man, after waiting forty years and traveling halfway around the world, will be content to look at his village from a distance of four miles and then go quietly away?

"You *can* apply for special permission," the travel agent said. "Possibly you may even receive it."

And if I don't, I see myself standing there at the top of the mountain, empty-handed. Never mind, I will slide down the bank and creep through the thicket at Batchuosoko, or I might climb up and circle around on the ridge, as I did so many times before, or I could follow the stream through the ravine. But one way or another, I will walk through my village. That I know.

"Make the reservation," I said to the agent.

Now came the next problem. The airline told me we can take only eighty-eight pounds of baggage between us.

"Eighty-eight pounds!" I said to my wife. "Do they expect a man gone forty years would return with less than a peddler's pack? Does that airline know how many relatives I have?"

"I think it very unlikely," Helena said, "since you don't know yourself. Before I buy anything in the way of presents, let's count again."

Now my family, I must admit, is a little complicated. When I was six, my mother died. My brother, David, who was not yet two, went to live with our Aunt Salome— *Mamedah*, we called her, which means "Father's Sister." She was a widow. In the first summer of her marriage, cholera spread through the village. In those times there were no doctors, at least not for poor people, and many died, among them Mamedah's husband, and after him, his brother and his brother's wife and two of their children. Left only was their baby, Sandro. Mamedah took this nephew for her own son, just as later she took our David.

All she had was a little vineyard, less than two acres, but by making wine and baking bread for the neighbors, she managed to keep herself and the two boys. Although Sandro was ten or twelve years older than David, he was a kind of extra brother to him and to me, too, when I went sometimes to visit my aunt.

For after my mother died, I stayed with my father, and he and I lived alone—alone, that is, except for our horse and my dogs, who kept me company when my father went away to work.

Years afterward, when I had already gone from home, my father married again. My stepmother, Nina, I saw many times, but my father's second family, born after I left Georgia, were all strangers to me. From letters, I knew I had two sisters, Maro and Leila, and two brothers, Alexander and Irvandis.

"For them," I told Helena, "I am nobody—only a name that Father, perhaps, sometimes spoke."

My brother David was married and had children. I expected to see him, of course, and his family, but who else? Father was dead, and Mamedah, too.

"But you must have other relatives," Helena said.

"No one will be left after all these years. Not Sandro, not my Aunt Maca that I danced with at her wedding when she married my Uncle Zacharia."

"Is she the one," Helena said, "that made the best of all pickled walnuts?"

"That was her mother. Never again in this world will I taste such kind of walnuts."

"I can see what I am going to need most," Helena said, getting out her notebook, "is a family tree."

"What use," I said, "if they are all gone?"

"You'll find somebody. Maybe your mother's youngest brother, the one who worked in stone and gave you your bear."

"My Uncle Georgi. No. He would be," I counted up, "a hundred, or at least ninety-five. I wish he lived to see how I carve stone."

"All the neighbors you've told me about," Helena said,

"just think, you'll see them. Teddua, the little boy who used to go with you for the water buffaloes, Bootla who was apprenticed with you, and the man that rose from the dead. . . ."

"He did *not*," I told Helena for the hundredth time, "rise from the dead. He waked up from a coma just as we were carrying his coffin into the church, so he came to his own funeral party and enjoyed himself, too."

I can never convince Helena this really happened, but for once she didn't argue the matter but only said, "He, at any rate, must still be alive, not to say immortal. You'll find lots of other old friends. Don't worry."

But I did worry. After a revolution and two wars, after all the years in between, who will be left? Would it be better not to go at all? Will I be a ghost, I asked myself, walking through an empty house?

Before I ever found an answer, it was too late to make any difference, for by this time we had flown over the Atlantic and across Europe, and we were taking off from the Moscow airport for Tbilisi.

Nothing to do now but wait and see what happened, so I filled my pipe, only to discover I had no matches.

"Ask the stewardess," Helena said, "or the man across the aisle. He is smoking a cigarette."

Now I face my first problem. What do I call him? Our customary way to address a stranger was to say *"Batono,"* which means "Prince," or for women, *"Kal Batono,"* "Lady Princess." But in a Communist country maybe this is now an insult. The term "Mr." or "Sir" we do not have. Do I say Comrade? Maybe Friend?

Before I could decide the man saw my cold pipe and offered me matches.

"Wish you?" he asked in English.

"Thank you," I said in Georgian.

He jumped as if I had stuck him with the point of a dagger. "You speak Georgian!"

"I do."

"And you speak without one trace of accent!"

"Naturally."

"But where did you learn?"

"The same place as you."

"As I?"

"At my mother's knee."

"But you speak English to the lady who is with you."

"My wife. She is an American."

"An American! How came she here?"

"With me. From the United States."

"When?"

"Yesterday."

"Yesterday! Impossible! And how long were you away from home?"

"Forty years."

"Forty! Forty years from home and not one word lost."

"Why should that surprise you?"

The man shook his head. "Now if boys go from Georgia to school in Moscow or to work in Samarkand, when they come back on vacation hardly they can remember our word for bread."

"Maybe *they* can afford to waste their language. I could not. It was all I had of home to take with me when I left."

"And you kept it well through all those years. But how could you leave home and go so far away?"

"I wanted to learn all about automobiles and how they were designed and made."

"You were a student?"

"No. It was 1918. I was a soldier tired of war."

"You achieved your ambition?"

"Not entirely. When I arrived in the United States, I spoke no English. I had to take whatever jobs I could find. I washed dishes, tarred roofs, shoveled scrap metal—"

"How many times you must have wished yourself back home again."

"Often and often, but finally I learned the language and went on the assembly line in an automobile factory—"

"And now you are an engineer and design the big cars with many horsepower?"

"No, I discovered factory life was not for me. I found another job selling box lunches to construction workers."

"Excellent. Always people want to eat—but at a table if possible. So I suppose eventually you opened a restaurant?"

"Yes, but it was too much like a factory. No chance to walk on grass, to see the sky, to hear the birds sing. Just as soon as we saved a little money, for by that time I was married, my wife and I bought a farm."

"What could be better. I can guess the rest. Like any Georgian you immediately set out a vineyard and sold your grapes to a winery."

"As it happened I raised tomatoes and sold them to a ketchup cannery. Meantime, my wife and I wrote a book about my experiences as an immigrant in the U.S.A."

"And it was a great success."

"We were satisfied."

"You wrote many more books?"

"Four or five."

"Then you are an author. Congratulations."

"Not exactly . . ."

"What then?"

"A sculptor. For the last twenty-five years that has been my profession. I carve in stone."

"But to be a sculptor you did not need to leave home at all."

"Who knows?"

"Well, in any case, you have returned and all is well. Now you must tell more about the United States of America. For a long time I am interested in this wonderful country, and I study its language. Does it have grapes? Good wine? Apples? Many lakes? Fast streams?"

In a few minutes I had a full audience around me—across, in front, and in back were two layers of men in every seat, and in the aisles as well, the stewardess stepping over them very good-naturedly while she served lunch. While we ate, I answered a hundred questions—what kind of fruit do we have, the size of a station wagon, are there still Indians, how long must a doctor go to school, the price of my suit, the size of our house, the names of the other Georgians in the United States, is there much difference between a Republican and a Democrat, and do I ever meet Mr. Duke Ellington.

Before I know it we are over the Caucasus, the great range that divides us from the rest of Europe.

The man across the aisle jumped up.

"Kal Batono, Kal Batono," he said to Helena, "please come over here and see below. Quickly, Kal Batono!"

We both looked out. On opposite sides, rising above the earth, above the very sky, were the great peaks of Kavkaz and Elbruz, covered with rosy pink snow.

After we had passed between the two mountains and the excitement was over, and we were back in our own seats, I remembered something.

"Excuse me," I said to the man across the aisle. "When you spoke to my wife a few moments ago, I noticed you still used "Kal Batono. . . .""

"Certainly. Why not?"

"Well, I thought that since—well, that nowadays 'Prince' and 'Lady Princess' would be omitted."

"Why? Just because we have a revolution is no reason to be impolite."

I looked out the window again. Below I could see houses on the steep mountainsides, and, then, catching the sun like an emerald, a huge lake, which I knew must be Basalete. No water in the world is so green. Soon we would be over Kobiantkari, but before I could find a landmark we were circling the Tbilisi airport.

"Look at all the people at the gate waving handkerchiefs and bouquets. There must be a commissar on board," Helena said. "Maybe the man in the black suit in the front seat."

"Rather the one with beard," I said. "He asked me to explain the Electoral College to him."

As our plane taxied in, the crowd broke through the wooden gate and rushed, it seemed to me, straight at the propellers.

The pilot neatly avoided them.

"He seems used to it," Helena said. "Perhaps reception committees are the natural hazard here."

Our flight was over. We waited now to see who *is* the commissar. Everybody else waited, too, including the man in the black suit and the one with the beard. But no commissar stood up.

Finally the stewardess came down the aisle and whispered a few words to me.

"She says," I told Helena, "that nobody will get off until we do."

"Why?"

"We're the guests. We must go first."

So down the steps we went.

"Now," I said to Helena, "I touch Georgian earth again."

But I spoke too soon, for I was caught up and swept away by a laughing, crying horde of people, and I realized whom the reception committee was for. Us!

Here was my brother David. We kissed and the years vanished, and after him came beautiful ladies and little children and men of all ages, but who were they?

My eyes were so full of tears I could not tell. Here was my stepmother in widow's black, yet when I turned, I saw her again as young as on her wedding day, her hair still as bright as copper in the sun.

Faces flashed before me. A young woman with dark curls and hazel eyes is my sister, but which one? No time to ask. Another beautiful lady with black hair and rosy cheeks kisses me. She, too, is my sister. And after her is a fair-haired, blue-eyed sister. How many sisters do I have? Or maybe it's a sister-in-law.

The boy who looks like a lyric poet is my nephew. But who are the two girls with notebooks and the man who wants to make me a long speech?

Helena, her arms filled with flowers, was surrounded, too, and even more bewildered than I. From time to time as she came near me she would ask, "Who is *this*?"

"Damned if I know," was all I could say before I was swept on.

At last I came to the edge of the crowd. There an old, old man waited for me. He took me in his arms and kissed me.

"At last, at last you came home." His eyes were full of tears. "Welcome."

Who could this be? My brother-in-law? Too old. An uncle? Too young. He dried his eyes and spoke again.

"Give me please checks for your suitcases." He was the baggage master.

The Intourist guide finally reached our side. It was arranged she would take us to our hotel to register.

"Immediately afterward," I told Helena, "we are going to Maro's house. The whole family will be there."

We rode along a highway bordered with double rows of apricot trees in bloom into Tbilisi, not the Tbilisi I knew, but a city with wide, clean streets, many parks, and new modern buildings along with refurbished old ones. Our hotel, one of the latter, was on Rustaveli Prospekt.

"Do you know it?" Helena asked me.

"Very well," I said, "from the outside. Often I wondered what it must be like inside."

When we had finally registered and were alone in our room, I looked around. A huge hall led into a living room twenty-five by twenty-five, not counting the alcove that held the grand piano. French windows along two walls opened on to balconies. I went out and looked down.

In a few minutes Helena joined me. "The bedroom is huge, too; the sheets and towels are handwoven linen; the bathroom has marble floors and walls; the plumbing, contrary to reports, works, but in the tub the spigots and drain are at opposite ends. Which way do you face?"

"I don't know. When I lived here, I never used—in fact, I never saw—a bathtub."

"Well, that problem can wait. What we'd better do now is see if we can sort out the people at the plane. Some spoke English. The pretty girl with the curls did. Do you know who she is?"

"No."

"Or the round old lady?"

"No."

"Or which one was Maro's husband?"

I shook my head. I was still looking around. Rustaveli Prospekt was below us. How many times I had walked along that street. First as a poor boy from the village without one kopeck in my pocket to spend for bread. Later, and scarcely better off, as a soldier tired of fighting wars no one could win. It seems as if I must still be standing there below on the corner watching this man above. Which me am I? The barefoot and hungry boy on the street below or the tourist from America in the hotel?

I see I am going to have a problem recognizing people, especially myself!

CHAPTER TWO

*B*efore we had a chance to unpack it was time to go to Maro's. She lived, she told me, in an "older" apartment built before World War II by her husband's union, the Transport Workers.

What the building looked like I couldn't judge, because when we arrived we found the entrance, the halls, the staircases lined with neighbors waiting to shake hands and welcome us. As for Maro's apartment it was, this day, one great table with an extension on to a balcony, and we sat on chairs, beds, trunks, boxes, and, in the case of the children, each other.

I began as best I could to sort out the family. There was David and his beautiful wife, Zina, and their youngest son, Dadico. Another boy, Levan, was in the service, and David's two oldest children were both married with families of their own. Could he, my little brother, really be a grandfather? Impossible! His face may have aged, but not his carefree spirit. Merry as ever—reciting snatches of poetry, playing tricks, telling jokes, most of them on me, producing presents from his pockets, singing, laughing, he made us all happy because he was.

Nina, my stepmother, had not really changed either. Her face was lined and her red, gold hair frosted white, but her eyes sparkled and she was still, at eighty, straight and spare and nearly as quick as ever.

Maro, the older of my sisters, looked exactly like her mother when first I saw her. No wonder at the plane I thought I glimpsed the past. The man in the gray uniform was Maro's husband, Jacob, the laughing girl was their daughter, Eterre, and their son, Ansor, the one who reminded me of a young John Gilbert.

Leila, my youngest sister, a pretty girl with dark curls and hazel eyes came and sat beside us. As yet unmarried, she lived with Maro and was a meteorologist. She was telling me of her work when a tall man walked in and embraced me.

"I could not come to the plane," he said, "but with all my heart I welcome you home."

"Do I know you?"

"No, but I know you. You have our father's face. I am your brother, Alexander."

With him was his wife, another Eterre, and their three little girls, too shy almost to whisper "Welcome home, Bdzea."

After Alexander came a beautiful woman in widow's black. Although she was young, scarcely forty I should have guessed, she wore the old headdress. This was the wife of my half-brother, Irvandis, who died in the first year of their marriage. Her name was Nina, but she was called in the family "Irvandis' wife" to distinguish her from my step-mother, perhaps, but, also, I think, to keep that much, at least, of Irvandis alive. Her son, Nougzari, twenty, who never saw his father, was with her, a nephew to be proud of, modest, unself-conscious, and sensible.

When the table and the hallway as far as I could see were filled with people, wine was poured and everyone fell silent.

All Georgian tables must have a *tamada*, a toastmaster, and Alexi, our youngest brother, was ours.

"This," he said, raising his glass, "is a great moment. Our eldest brother, now the head of our family, has come home, and with all our hearts we welcome him—"

Then in a kind of poetry he told of the years that had passed —of the wars and the revolution, of sorrow and suffering, of joy and victory, of death and partings, of marriages and births.

"—and through it all," Alexander turned to me, "you were never forgotten. Always when we filled our glasses we drank to our brother far away. Now we drink to him come safely home at last."

To answer Alexi's toast was not easy. The best I could I told them about working in steel mills in Pittsburgh, automobile plants in Detroit, and factories in California. I told how I became an American citizen and a farmer in Pennsylvania. I told how I met and married Helena and how she put the story of my experiences into a book that many people in the United States and in other countries, too, read. I told how I began to carve, first in wood and then in stone. I told of the lonely times and then of the happiest life a man could have.

Many, many more toasts followed. To my new country and to my old, to friendship, to understanding, to peace, to those absent from our midst, to us, around the table, at last together.

Before I could drain my glass to that sentiment we were in the middle of a family argument with everybody talking at me, explaining, interrupting, contradicting. All I could do was listen.

"What's the difficulty?" Helena asked when she could put a word in.

"A long-standing disagreement. As the oldest it seems I'm the chief justice. I've just heard both sides of the case. Now I'm supposed to hand down an opinion."

"About what?"

"About Ansor. Should he or should he not change his name."

"What will you say?"

"The truth. That I don't care."

"If you do that, then you'll offend everyone. At least take one side or the other and please half."

I thought a few minutes.

"In a serious matter such as this," I said, "only one thing is possible. Ansor must decide entirely for himself without *any* advice from anyone."

This was such an original idea that it had to be talked over, and soon we were all friends again except, of course, with Ansor who was to blame for making so much trouble.

Many, many more toasts we drank and between times we ate, and, thanks to my sisters' skill, each dish was better than the next—scallions, broad-leafed cress, and bouquets of tarragon to tuck into flat bread, salt cheese, roast chicken with sauce from wild sour plums, pickled tomatoes, white fish, lamb baked with quinces, eggplant caviar, hot corn bread, and still the dishes came and the toasts went on. We laughed and sang and wept and laughed again.

By the time we had come to our *Quellas Mindas,* the last toast, for all the saints in heaven or on earth, it was very late. The streets were deserted and the city dark as we rode back to our hotel.

The door was locked, but a sleepy watchman let us in. No elevator service, so we tiptoed up the staircase and down the hall. At the end of the corridor just outside our door waited three men in identical dark suits and shirts so white they gleamed.

"Who are they?" Helena whispered. "Policemen? Or maybe robbers?"

I went ahead, and as I came closer I saw around the corner sitting on sofas were two ladies and five or six young people. That was a relief. I don't think policemen, or for that matter thieves, even in Georgia, take their families on the job.

Now they all came toward me. It must be some kind of delegation—and from the theater or moving pictures very probably, since they were all so fine in appearance, in dress, and in manner.

The man and then the two ladies with tears in their eyes kissed me, and after them a beautiful girl and four boys came forward and they, too, embraced us.

The oldest, twenty-five perhaps, tall and dark with flashing eyes, said, "Since we were old enough to hear your name we waited to greet you. Now this moment we lived for has come, and we rejoice."

"Who are they?" Helena said.

"I don't know. Not yet."

"We won't find out standing in a hallway. Invite them in."

I did. We all sat down, and the younger boys spoke in turn to me.

"What do they say?" Helena asked.

"That they appreciate what I did for them. It made a great difference in their lives, and never a day passed they did not in their hearts thank me."

Now Helena is ready to cry, too.

"How wonderful! What was it you did?"

"I don't know that either."

I looked from one to the other of our visitors. The youngest boy, fair hair, strong-boned, smiled at me. And then I guessed and I went to him.

"You have the face of Mamedah's Sandro—"

Very shy, yet very proud, the boy said, "I have Grandfather's name, too, Uncle."

"Grandfather?" I turned to the three men, "Can it be possible you are Sandro's children? I left you, Samabah, playing knucklebones in the dooryard and you, Giorgi and Challico, still babies, and now you have children of your own!"

"And grandchildren," Samabah said. "My daughter has two daughters."

His wife Susanah, he said, was not there to greet us because she was in the hospital. . . . "But now she hears you came she feels already better."

Slowly we sorted everybody out.

Giorgi and his wife, Vera, a slender, graceful woman with great dark eyes, had one son, Giorgi, called Gigola, a college student. Young Sandro was Samabah's son, and his older boy, an electrical engineer, was there, too. He spoke enough English to tell Helena his name was Robeso.

"Robeso?" Helena said. "Is that a Georgian name?"

"Oh, no, before I was born my mother was reading your great English classic, and she named me for its hero, Robeso Cruzo."

Challico, the youngest brother, and his blonde, blue-eyed Elena, both bubbling with laughter introduced their son, Waja, only seventeen but six feet tall, and their daughter, Gula, who looked as if she might be a model but was a construction engineer.

Now I named them all over to Helena, and each one kissed her again.

"Sandro—your father would be eighty-six . . ." I said. "If only I had come in time to see him once again. To sit with him in the arbor—"

"He *is* eighty-six," Samabah said. "He lives."

"And in good health and makes wine from Mamedah's grapes, and he waits to see you," Challico said.

What better news could we hear? Sandro alive and well and blessed with a family like this. At once we made plans on how and when we would go to Mukhran all together to visit him.

So our first day ended.

"People keep asking me," I said to Helena when we were alone, "do I see any improvements. This much I could say. I left home half an orphan and I come back to enough family to satisfy any reasonable man."

"True," Helena said, "but I still don't know what these dear ones were thanking you for so warmly."

"Oh, that was because I taught my brother David how to drive a car when I came back from war, and as soon as they grew up, David taught them."

CHAPTER THREE

*E*arly next morning I was scarcely awake when I heard a small knock at the door. It was my brother David's son, Dadico. Behind him, carrying a large tray of breakfast, came another boy, also about seventeen. They greeted me, set the table, cut the cheese bread, peeled oranges, and filled glasses with hot tea, and sat down with pleased expressions to watch us eat.

"I recognize Dadico," Helena said, "but is the other one from room service or a blood relative?"

"Neither, exactly. He's David's wife's sister's son. I guess you could call him a self-elected nephew."

"What's his name?"

"Ura."

Hearing himself mentioned, Ura rose, kissed Helena's hand, and sat down again.

"Give me my notebook," Helena said. "I might as well add him to the family tree. Where, by the way, did they bring breakfast from? Home?"

"No, they bought it, but they won't let me pay them for it."

"At least they must help us eat it!"

After enough refusals to be polite, the boys joined us at the table.

"What's that?" Helena said, pointing to a plate.

"Fish. Filet of trout, I think, with a sauce of barberries."

"And that? Just out of the oven apparently."

"*Hadje Pore*. Sulgule cheese folded into dough and then baked."

"I think," Helena said after she tried both dishes, "I had better start a recipe section next to the genealogy chart."

When we finished, the boys removed the tray and came back with the morning newspaper for me and a packet of postcards, colored views of the city, for Helena. At intervals they vanished to reappear with stamps for the postcards, matches, a bouquet, extra vases for the other flowers we had accumulated along the way, and pots of fresh tea. Between trips they sat in two straight chairs against the wall and thought, I guess, about what else they could go out and get for us.

"Don't they work—or go to school?" Helena asked me.

"Yes, but it seems they took their vacation now."

Someone knocked, and Dadico and Ura hastened to the door. It was Maro with some ripe persimmons for our breakfast, and after her came David and Zina with some hot corn bread, and then Alexi and Eterre, carrying what looked like a jar of topazes but proved to be quince preserves. What to do with this bounty was solved by the arrival of a man who had translated our first book for publication in Georgia, a reporter, with a photographer, for an interview, and a delegation of three students who invited us to speak at the university.

Dadico and Ura removed coats and hung them in the closet, brought forward chairs, adjusted window shades, relaid the table with fresh plates and silver, and produced, apparently from a bottomless well of it in the corridor, more fresh tea.

"I feel as if I had a footman and a butler at my command," I told Helena.

"Or two genies out of a bottle . . ."

After the reporter, students, and translator had departed, everybody started talking at once, trying to tell me forty years of family history in as many minutes. I would be there yet, hearing in one ear the details of my Uncle Zacharia's funeral, ". . . a very rainy day it was, which made us weep all the more. . . ." and in the other ear a description of Maro's wedding, ". . . over one hundred people expected and where were the eggplants. . . ." except we had an appointment at twelve o'clock with the Intourist representatives at their office downstairs in the hotel. There I would be told if I am allowed to go to my village—or not.

A few minutes before the hour we set out with Dadico going ahead to announce our arrival and Ura acting as a rear guard to pick us up if we fell down the marble staircase.

The manager turned out to be a handsome young woman named Miss Cecilia, with a mass of black curls, luminous eyes, fluent and graceful in English, and, I soon discovered, briskly efficient.

"Whom do you wish to meet? Artists? Writers? What do

you wish to see? Schools? Hospitals? Farms? Museums? Theater? Opera? Ballet? Where do you wish to go? Sochi? Mtsketa?"

"All of those, yes, but most particularly I want to go to Kobiantkari."

"The countryside is very beautiful now that spring has come."

"And to Muhkran where my aunt lived . . ."

"Flowers will be blooming everywhere."

"And to my brother's in Kutais."

"Kutais? But no Americans have ever gone to Kutais."

"We will enjoy to be the first ones."

"But regretfully as yet, there is no Intourist Hotel in Kutais."

"Nevertheless," I said firmly, "I would like to go there and to my aunt's village, but most particularly to my own, Kobiantkari."

"In that case I will make inquiry of the Director General."

And by the time you receive an answer, I thought to myself, we'll be back in the United States. But all I said was "When?"

"At once. Come we will go to his office. Next door."

There Mr. Palavandishvily, a portly, dignifed man, received us, and we were all seated around a long mahogany table.

Was our health and that of our friends and family here and in the U. S. of A. good, our trip pleasant?

"Yes, except that I . . ."

"Your accommodations are comfortable?"

"Yes, but . . ."

"Your schedule satisfactory?"

"I want to . . ."

Before I could make my request, a cut-glass goblet, a fruit plate, and a silver knife were set before each of us, and the same moment a large basket of fruit, a plate of cakes, and a bottle of wine appeared in the middle of the table. The Director, after filling our glasses, made a most polite toast of welcome, to which I naturally replied. Thereafter, we also drank to the U.S.A., the U.S.S.R., to peace and friendship, to culture in general. Meantime, Miss Cecilia peeled, segmented, and ate a large ripe orange without spilling a drop of juice while translating the conversation for Helena's benefit.

When the toasts were finished and I had answered all the usual questions about America and my life there for Mr. Palavandishvily, he said, "You will find many changes in Kobiantkari, I think."

"Then we may go there?"

"Of course. Why not?"

"And to Mukhran. . . ?"

"If you wish—a most pleasant drive."

"And Kutais?"

"That is too far for one day. You would need to stay overnight. We have not an Intourist Hotel there as yet, but something can be arranged."

"When can I go?"

"Whenever you please. We have nothing to hide. Take a guide if you wish, or go alone. There are trains, buses, planes. You will find your way. You can speak." He shook my hand warmly. "I congratulate you. Forty years gone from home, you tell me, and I see that not one word you lost." He shook my hand again.

Back at the hotel the source of the instant meals that had appeared all morning was revealed. On every floor was a buffet, a combination of snack bar, delicatessen, cocktail lounge, and room-service depot, where one could buy wine, fruit juices, tea, cakes, cold ham, cheese, and bread over the counter and order hot dishes sent up by dumb-waiter from the main restaurant, a plan of such originality and value that it more than balanced, as Helena said, the reversed bathroom fixtures. From this buffet we found a splendid lunch had been assembled in our rooms, where everyone was still waiting for us.

"Good news!" I announced. "Best news! I can go to my village."

Nobody seemed surprised, or pleased, or, to tell the truth, very interested.

"What's the hurry to go to the village?" my sister asked. "Everything's here. Museums, opera, ballet, shops."

"Village is the same as always," Alexi said.

"But that's just what I want to—"

"Oh, there are many changes," his wife said. "A new school and a clinic, but there are much larger ones here."

"It's friends and neighbors I want to see."

"We'll invite them to Tbilisi."

"And our house beneath the beech."

"The old house is gone long ago. Father had a much better house closer to Dushet. With water from a pipe. And electric lights."

Our house gone! This was a shock to me. For a minute I thought perhaps I should forget the whole thing. But no. I knew I could not.

"The village is more than any one house in it," I said, "even my own. I still want to go there."

"You'll probably get lost," Alexi laughed. "I will have to hunt for you."

"Never."

"One day we will all go together; that will be best," my sister Leila said, "but first you must see the sights in Tbilisi."

"And visit me in Kutaisi," David said. "I will show you our huge automobile factory and the forestry school and the new Folk Opera House and the ancient monastery at Gelati—"

To all that was proposed I agreed.

"What use to argue?" I said later to Helena. "Nevertheless, we're going to Kobiantkari one way or another the first chance we get."

"Of course, but it's only polite meantime to look at all the modern things here everybody has worked so hard to accomplish."

So immediately after lunch we all set off, eight of us in the party, to go to the top of Mount St. David, which rises sharply from the center of the city.

The funicular railway to the summit was not running, we learned. Should we take the autobus? If so, would Number 4 or Number 6 be preferable? Several bystanders were consulted. Some said 4, others 6, while a dedicated minority rejected both in favor of the Number 3 line.

A lady asked Helena her opinion, and when she did not understand her rapid Georgian, repeated it again in Russian. When Helena still looked bewildered, she pantomimed sympathetically, "Are you deaf and dumb?"

"Americanski," Helena said.

"American? From the United States?" The autobus controversy was forgotten, and we held a small reception on the curbing, answering the usual questions until the Number 8 bus arrived, which, it turned out, was the the one we really wanted, and our party climbed on. We wound through the city, then up the steep hillside, where apricot trees bloomed against dark pines.

"Planted in pockets of rock," my sister-in-law Eterre said, "and for two years Young Pioneers carried a bucket of water to each tree every day."

At the summit was a broad plateau with gardens, lawns, and walks around an airy pavilion that provided a view of the entire city twenty-two hundred feet below.

Tbilisi lies in a narrow valley. Houses climb the mountain-sides. We could see the copper roofs of the old dwellings shining in the sun. Scattered among them were scores of modern buildings—hospitals, schools, libraries, whole blocks of apartments, the university complex, hotels, a mushroom-topped sportdrome, and the steel skeletons of more to come. Parks dotted the city, and cutting across one end was a swath of tree-bordered greenland a mile wide and ten miles long. My head was spinning on a swivel to see it all.

"Look over there," said David, pointing eastward with a proprietary air. "That is our Inland Sea. Did you ever expect an ocean to come to Tbilisi?"

Sure enough, a great expanse of water glittered in what I remembered as dry hills.

"An ocean with miles of beaches, and swimming and boats to ride around in, and a restaurant on the water where we'll go to eat fish," Maro said. "Nothing like *that* in the village!"

"This is only a quick view, but don't worry," my brother Alexander reassured me. "We will take you to see all these things right on the spot."

"We've already made a program," Leila told me. "To-morrow we go first to . . ."

Helena, who had wandered off by herself, came back to say I must see the formal garden on the other side of the pavilion.

"There's a huge globe with the continents bedded out in contrasting blooms and a sputnik full of pansies lifting off from the U.S.S.R. The outer park is carpeted in sweet violets, and when I asked a militia man if I might have one, he and two strangers picked me this huge bouquet. People are very kind."

"That," I said, "seems to be the main difficulty. I wonder if I ever will manage to break away and get to Kobiantkari?"

"Be patient," Helena said. "You've waited forty years. Another few days can't make that much difference."

$\mathcal{S}$o, although I wanted to see the village more than anything else, my brothers and sisters finally persuaded
me to wait until a day when they could all arrange to
go, too. Meantime, there was plenty to see on every
side, and my relatives, the Intourist guides, and even
total strangers were determined to show it to us.

Tbilisi is an old city, one of the oldest in the world.
In its fifteen hundred years it has been forty times
destroyed and forty-one times rebuilt. But never, I
think, have there been more changes than in the last
quarter century.

The Tbilisi I left in 1921 was, to tell the truth, a
crowded dirty place with neither a public-water,
electric, nor sewage system. The cobbled streets were
narrow, a donkey-width across and purposely made

crooked to deflect arrows, for Georgia was always a battle-
ground.

There was one hospital, grim enough, if you went inside,
to scare you well again, no free schools, and only a few pri-
vate ones, and more churches than God himself would want
to count.

Through the town ran the Kura River, a broad sluggish
stream full of filth and trash. In summer drought it slowed
to a trickle and left stagnant pools where mosquitoes bred,
so almost everyone had malaria.

Now I found the Kura rechanneled into a narrow, fast,
clean river with embankments on either side, linked with
fine apartments. Streets were widened into boulevards and
planted with trees and flowers. Now new hospitals, schools,
public buildings and housing rose on every side, with more
under way. A walk in any direction usually turned into an
obstacle course around excavations, across open trenches,
between piles of sand, gravel, and lumber.

"In the United States people would fall over or into this
stuff," Helena said, "and sue the city, but here it seems to
be regarded as a kind of ornamental feature in the land-
scape."

True to their promise my family took us on a round of
sightseeing. We went to the museum with its treasure room
full of the work of the ancient goldsmiths and potters; we
attended the theaters and opera; we heard concerts and saw
the ballet *Otello*—so beautiful that Shakespeare himself
would have applauded.

One day the Artists' Union invited us to a reception to
meet painters and sculptors and see their work. On another
day we went to the Writers' Union. When I lived in Georgia,

few people could read. Now I learned there is almost 100 per cent literacy, and the eight publishing houses in the republic issue seventeen million volumes a year. A popular author, the president of the Writers' Union told me, may sell a quarter million copies of a title.

"This I can hardly believe," I said to Helena as we were walking back to the hotel "since there are probably less than three and a half million Georgians all together."

"Even more incredible are the one hundred fifty periodicals they publish. People must read day and night."

Ahead of us we saw a long queue waiting on the sidewalk.

"Let's stop and see what's for sale," Helena said. "It must be some great rarity."

As we went up to look in the door, I could hear murmurings behind us.

"Be kind enough to await your turn."

"We should all remember to behave in a constructive manner."

"That means us," I said to Helena. So we went back to the end of the line.

The man just ahead of us wished us good day.

"At last," he smiled happily at us, "after three years what we were waiting for is here."

"So it seems," I said, "but could you tell me what it is?"

"You are joking. Surely you know?"

"No, I don't."

"Then why do you wait?"

"To find out."

"Ah, so you are a speculator. . . ."

In another minute I am afraid that I will have to tell again the story of my life, and frankly I am beginning to get rather

tired of myself, so I said, "Certainly I am not a speculator.
I have been away. I came from Moscow only a few days
ago."

"From Moscow. No wonder. Well, we wait to go into the
bookstore."

"For what?"

"The new volume of Noniashvili's poetry is on sale. Unless
those before us are very greedy, you and I have every chance
to buy a copy."

"I guess I have to change my mind," I said to Helena,
"maybe they *do* sell a quarter million copies of a title."

"It's a sight to remember," she said. "I don't think anybody
stood in line to buy a book in the U.S. since Dickens's *Oliver
Twist* appeared in monthly installments."

We visited schools and saw the children, the little girls in
black pinafores and white blouses with big butterfly bows
bobbing on their braids, the boys in neat uniforms, carrying
book satchels. We heard them recite and looked at their work
—maps, notebooks, compositions, drawings. We stopped at
the Young Pioneer Club rooms after regular classes were
over and watched ballerinas, musicians, potters, artists, car-
penters, and photographers in the making.

In one school the principal asked me to speak to some of
the older students. Introducing me, he said, "Here is our
countryman who was gone from home forty years, and yet
you will see not one word of his language did he lose. Let
all of you, when far away, remember to do so well."

"If I hear another time how well I still speak Georgian,"
I said to Helena, "I fear I will be so puffed with pride that
I will float like a balloon figure in a Thanksgiving parade."

Fortunately, I was spared such a fate. That same afternoon

we were scheduled to give a short lecture to the English Language Department at the university. When all four hundred students with their professors were in their seats. I stood up and began my talk, naturally in English. Everybody listened intently, but as I went on speaking, I could see their bright, intelligent faces turning blanker and blanker. Some pressed forward to hear better, so I spoke louder, and they looked even more bewildered. I realized they could not understand a single word I was saying, and suddenly I guessed why. Never before had they heard anyone speak broken English. Immediately I switched to Georgian with the excuse that it gave me pleasure to use it after so many years away, and immediately all the faces smiled again and the ears understood.

After our speeches were over, there was a nice reception for us, with fruits and wine and cake and speeches and toasts, and a thousand questions about the United States. A student read an original poem in English, too, and pretty young girls filled our arms with flowers and our pockets full of chocolates, and when it was time to go, they escorted us all the way to the street.

As he bid us good-bye, one of the professors said, "Please excuse me, but your wife's English seems a bit easier to understand than yours. Is this a matter of regional differences in the U.S.A.?"

"Not exactly," I said. "English is her native tongue, and she learned it at home and at school, but mine I picked up from Poles in the Ambridge Steel Mills, from Chinese storekeepers in California, from Pennsylvania Dutch farmers— wherever and however I could—and it is what you might call immigrant American."

After that, I stuck to Georgian and let Helena handle all
the people who wanted to practice their English.

Every night we had the pleasure of another party in a
different house. Alexander's wife Eterre roasted a turkey
with nut sauce, and Maro made me my favorite *kinkhali,*
ground meat in noodle dough, pinched tightly and boiled in
bouillon and for dessert her famous *murahbah,* candied
fruits in syrup. After each toast the young people sitting
together at the end of the table would start one of the old
songs, and soon the rooms were filled with voices in chorus.

On Saturday, as we had planned, Samabah, Georgi, Challico, and their families called for us after breakfast, and we
set out for Muhkran, driving along a road bordered with
double rows of apricot trees. Within the hour we were
there.

"Can I believe my eyes?" I said to Giorgi as we came in
sight of the gate. "Do I see the green summer apple tree
still stands?"

"Still stands and bears," Georgi said proudly.

"And the same willow? How many baskets we wove from
its branches."

"Always there since I can remember," Samabah said.

"And if not the *very* same willow, then a son or a grandson
of the old tree," Challico told me.

We turned into the yard and stopped beneath the great
arbor, and there, on the long veranda of the old stone house,
Sandro waited for me as so often he had before.

Of course, we talked of all that had happened since we
parted, and of Mamedah and the old days when we were
boys. Sandro, although his step was slow, took me all around
the farm. I think he wanted me to see it was in as good heart

as when Mamedah lived. Every inch was cultivated; the grapes pruned tightly, the clippings stacked in neat piles to use for broiling *m'tswade* and for baking bread in Mamedah's own outdoor brick oven.

Vegetables grew along the paths with herbs tucked in the corners; a double row of fruit trees bordered the road. Under the house in the cool stone cellar apples were heaped in bins and golden pears and medlars ripened on slatted shelves.

Indoors, Vera, Elena, and Susanah had been showing Helena the cupboards full of jams, fruit in syrup, honey, pickled walnuts, and dried fruits. Now they were explaining to her partly in pantomime how to make *chuchkella*, our fruit candy.

"You crack nuts and string them." Vera demonstrated.

"And make a syrup of grape juice and just a little flour." Elena stirred the air vigorously so it would not burn.

"Then dip the strings in the syrup and hang them up to drain. Next day dip again . . . and again. When they are dry, you slice—" Susanah cut a real *chuchkella*, "like this and eat."

We all did.

After that the ladies took the big pitchers from the dresser and found one for Helena.

"We have water now piped to the house," Vera explained, "but for drinking and for tea we still think the best comes fresh from the river. So let us go there now."

As they walked along the street word spread, and women came out to greet Helena as she passed and tell her they knew and loved my aunt.

"Each one had her special link to Mamedah," Helena told me when they came back. "One said, 'She nursed me when I was sick.' Another said, 'She was my oldest son's godmother.' 'She baked the best bread in Muhkran!' 'She taught me how to make pickles.' "

Little boys and girls followed them all the way, and at the river the boys vied for the honor of wading in and filling the pitchers from the fast deep center of the stream and then carrying them home. By the time they came back, it was a procession of thirty people.

Meantime, at home Challico and Samabah moved tables and chairs out of the arbor, and Giorgi got a shovel and carefully, carefully dug away the earth that covered the mouth of the great quevre, the earthen amphora full of wine that lay buried there.

"Ever since you left, Mamedah kept this filled with wine at least five years old, waiting for you to come, and I have done the same," Sandro said.

And now here I am.

Slowly, so not one drop of earth would fall in, the top was removed, and Challico dipped the first glass for me, the second for his father, and we drank to Mamedah who had enough love to sustain three families and last four generations.

After we had a feast, more neighbors came, and we sat around the table, older people at the head, the younger ones grouped together at the end. We sang the toasts—*Mhraval Jahmeeay*—"May you live a thousand years in joy." We sang heroic songs, "What Does a Man Leave When He Goes to War?" We sang romantic songs, "Suliko" and

> Fly, butterfly, fly,
> Fly thru the air above,
> Fly, butterfly, fly,
> Fly to the one I love.

We sang nonsense songs—making up verses about each other and roaring the chorus. Last of all we began the song of home, "Georgia is a garden green—" our voices rising over the walls, over the vines, out to reach the stars.

CHAPTER FIVE

My brother David had to go home to Kutaisi, a city two hundred miles west of Tbilisi, but before he left he made me promise we would join him there a day or two later.

"Don't fail me," he said, "because I will make a party and show you to all my friends."

Since there was no official Intourist hotel in Kutaisi, I asked Miss Cecilia where we might stay.

"No problem," she said. "Near Kutaisi, only a five-kopeck trolley bus fare away is Skaltupa, a most famous health resort with hot springs and many sanitariums. I will arrange for you to stay in one of them, the largest and best one. You will enjoy it."

"A spa!" Helena said. "What could be better? We'll take the baths and drink the water that always smells like rotten eggs and come back twenty years younger and twenty pounds thinner."

"What's the name of the sanitarium?" I asked.

She gave us the name and address, and as soon as we had a confirmed flight I sent a telegram to the manager and one to my brother telling them when we would arrive.

Late the next day we set out for Kutaisi on a local plane that was as cosy as a country bus. There were several women with shopping baskets, two men who set up a chess game, an army officer, his wife, three children and their well-behaved German shepherd, and directly across the aisle from us, an old man, a farmer by the look of his boots and work clothes.

As the plane took off, he closed the window curtains and then his eyes. "I am riding first time," he said to me, "—and maybe last. Who knows?"

The stewardess came through. "Fasten your seat belts, please." She touched the old farmer's arm. "Comrade, be kind enough to fasten your seat belt."

"Why?"

"For your protection, Comrade. So you won't fall."

"Fall?" he laughed. "Where is there to fall—except to the floor of the plane?"

Emboldened by his own logic, he opened his eyes and found the courage to peek through a slit in the curtains.

I looked out our window. Below us black fields, newly turned, were like a vast chocolate cake iced with a criss-crossing of orchards in glistening white bloom.

"Hmm," said the farmer. "Whatever collective is below us has more plowed than we do in Alazani. But then perhaps we had more rain. We will catch up with them." He turned to me. "Where do you go?"

"Kutaisi. And you?"

"I go to Sukhumi to see my son. He is in the army. This morning was a telegram from him saying 'Come at once.' Nothing more. What does it mean? Who can say?"

This news passed the length of the plane over the sympathetic nervous system. Everyone had an immediate explanation to offer. Including me.

"Homesick," I said.

"No. He is a man and gone from home two years."

"Sick?" a lady suggested.

"Accident?" said her friend.

"No, or an army doctor signs the telegram."

"He drank too much and is in the guardhouse," the chess player said.

"For shame! For shame!" two elderly ladies exclaimed in unison.

Helena, who had somehow managed to follow the conversation, added, "Surely never that."

The farmer, however, seemed inclined to settle for this possibility. "It could be," he nodded his head. "He is still young and perhaps foolish enough to drink bad wine."

"Maybe your son plans to get married," the second chess player said, "and wants your blessing."

Here was an explanation that won instant approval from all the passengers. The farmer was delighted.

"Exactly, exactly. Why did I not think of that before? My son has found a girl, a very pretty girl. . . ."

". . . one with the higher education," the lady across the aisle added.

". . . and they will be married," said her friend almost ready to weep with joy.

". . . and I shall have grandchildren who come to visit me," the old man concluded happily.

The passengers beamed with as much pleasure as if they were toasting the happy couple.

It was dark when we came down in Kutaisi. Another plane from Sochi was just leaving for Tbilisi, and the station was crowded. We stood by the gate expecting momentarily to see my brother or my nephew waiting for us. Half an hour, forty-five minutes passed; no one came. I went to the desk and inquired where we could get a taxi into town.

No taxi was available. These were the last planes of the day. The airport closed in ten minutes. I explained my problem in turn to the assistant ticket agent, his chief, the plane dispatcher, and, finally, the director of the airport. Together, they explored the reason for a lack of a welcoming delegation.

"Slow telegraph service."

"Wrong address on your telegram."

"Absence from home of your relatives."

"Illness . . . but no, why borrow trouble?"

"I feel like the old man on the plane," I said to Helena. "Maybe my nephew got married this afternoon to a beautiful girl. . . ."

"With the higher education," Helena said, "but if that were so, the whole wedding party would be here."

As to a taxi, I was told that one could be called, but it would take almost an hour for it to drive out from town.

"However, before we do that," the director said, "let us wait a few minutes. Surely someone comes late for the plane that is already gone, and you can take *his* taxi back to town."

As if on cue, two men, one with a suitcase, dashed in.

"The Tbilisi plane?"

"Gone," said the clerk.

"Gone," said the dispatcher.

The director said nothing, but pointed beyond the horizon and shook his head.

The new arrivals turned to each other.

"Too late!"

"Too late!"

The one with the suitcase added, "And after my friend here brought me all the way in his car. Now what to do? I must be in Tbilisi tonight without fail."

"No more planes until morning," said the dispatcher.

"In that case, I must be in Tbilisi tomorrow without fail." The man picked up his suitcase.

"Wait a moment," said the director. "These visitors wish to go to Skaltupa and perhaps, since you have available the car, you would be so kind . . ."

"To Skaltupa? With pleasure, certainly. A beautiful place." He turned to us. "Soon you will be restored to perfect health."

He shook our hands and introduced himself and his friend to us and to the airport staff. We said our farewells, shook hands again, and off we drove.

"It's so late we'd better not try to find David tonight," Helena said. "Let's go directly to the sanitarium."

"To what sanitarium do you go?" our driver inquired.

"*That* is the question," I said to Helena. "I've completely forgotten the name."

"So have I, if I ever knew it."

"Was it Mountain View? No. Valley View? Something View, I'm sure."

"All health resorts have view in their name. It's probably a universal principle in medicine. All I remember about this one is Miss Cecilia saying it was the largest and the best."

I passed this description on the driver.

"But all are large, all are excellent. Which in particular?"

I explained our predicament.

"A simple matter, we will drive around and show you all the sanitariums and then you and the Lady Princess, your wife, will make your selection."

After an extended tour around the area and a short description of the advantages of this dining room, that garden, this bath house, that veranda, we chose what looked to be the most imposing building and went in.

It was almost midnight and the halls were hushed. We explained ourselves to a nurse on duty in the hall.

"Certainly you are expected here," she said when she learned my name. "But you do not come until tomorrow," she said. "Ten o'clock your telegram reads."

"Ten o'clock tonight."

"But there is no ten o'clock at night; only in the morning can it be ten o'clock. When it is past meridian, it is not ten but twenty-two o'clock—for planes and trains. I hope this does not have an adverse effect upon you. You must be so very tired, so very hungry. Come, I will make you comfortable at once."

In five minutes we were settled in a pleasant room; in ten minutes there was a knock on the door, and a girl brought in a tray covered with a starched white cloth.

"A snack only," she whispered. "The kitchen is closed. You must sleep very late in the morning and recover your spirits after all your troubles. Then you will have a good breakfast."

We uncovered the tray. Sliced ham, two kinds of cheese, six hardboiled eggs, two glasses of sour cream, a loaf of fresh bread, a mold filled with a rich sponge pudding, a small cake, and a pat of sweet butter shaped into a calla lily with parsley foliage, and a kettle of boiling water for tea.

The same maid brought breakfast in the morning. "You feel better? You have breathed our pure air? You have slept well? You found your bed comfortable? You would like another pillow?"

While she questioned us, she set out a platter of cold sturgeon, a bowl of sour cream, a dish of radishes, another of raw spinach, brown bread, sweet butter, a crisp pastry with a glazed top, a teapot, and plugged an electric kettle into an outlet.

"Begin," she said, "while I go, one, two, three for your omelet."

Before we could protest, she vanished, to return with an omelet so hot she must have cooked it in the corridor.

"Explain to her, please," Helena said, "that we are going to spend all day every day with your brother, and we don't eat breakfast here. Nor lunch, nor dinner, nor afternoon tea, nor supper, nor snacks, nor collations, nor any other word that describes a meal."

I did the best I could to make it clear, but the maid only smiled.

"Never fear," she said. "Soon your health will improve, and you will feel hungry again. Meantime we shall try to think of some little thing to rouse your appetite."

On our way out of the sanitarium the floor clerk, another maid, several fellow guests, and finally the director, each in turn, inquired for our health and had to be assured that we found our room, our mattress, the number of pillows, the fresh air, and the food satisfactory.

With the director I was firm. "Nothing more to eat, however, except a glass of tea for breakfast."

"We shall see."

"And we would like to take the baths."

"About that, too, we shall inquire."

We took the trolley bus to David's and found him just leaving to meet us at the 10:00 A.M. plane. The story in all of its detail and our deliverance called for a small celebration, and Zina set out a second breakfast of cheese bread, green beans baked with eggs, and a plateful of freshly pulled scallions.

While we ate, Zina drew up our schedule with all the efficiency of an Intourist guide.

"Today you will see the city. Tonight all the relatives, my sisters and brothers, and their families will come here for a party. Tomorrow we go to Gelati, and afterward we have another party for our friends and neighbors, and the next day. . . ."

"We go home," I said, "and you go with us, for Sunday we all go to Kobiantkari. This time without fail."

Somehow we stretched the hours and did all Zina had planned. One of David's friends toured us around the city in his taxi. We saw silk and furniture and leather factories, a hydroelectric station, the museum, and two parks all before noon, when Zina announced we would go to her mother's for lunch.

"She is ninety," she said, "and cannot leave her bed. She feels so sad she cannot be with us tonight, and this will give her some of the pleasure of the party."

We found Zina's mother waiting for us, propped up on snowy pillows, wearing a frilled cap and gown. She had a face like a winter apple, shrunken and full of wrinkles, but still rosy. We pushed the table to her bedside, and Zina set out pickled eggplants stuffed with hot peppers, goat cheese, white fish in a sauce of tomatoes, silver herrings sliced on a bed of scarlet radishes, a bowl of boiled potatoes, and a bottle of the dry red wine from grapes that grow only on the hills around Kutaisi.

Gradually the room began to fill with relatives, neighbors, until quite a party was assembled.

Zina's mother, whom we called *Bidzula,* which means "Honored Aunt," wanted to hear all Helena could tell her about everyday life in the United States. Helena explained washing machines, dryers, electric mixers, juicers, blenders, with all the enthusiasm of an appliance salesman on TV.

Bidzula asked very shrewed questions. "Some clothes are dirtier than others. How does the washer know when its work is finished and it shall stop?"

Helena explained about automatic switches, cycles, and repairmen until I think we could have signed Bidzula up for a fully automated household—all except the freezer and the dryer. She had the freezer described twice and then shook her head.

"It must look like a large coffin, and in any case, frozen food could never taste so well as fresh. As for the dryer, it is better, I think, to hang clothes outdoors in the garden so they have the perfume of the sun."

Lunch lasted so long that Bidzula's grandchildren came home from school and were given tastes of everything on the table. After more toasts and a few songs a tray heaped with fruit was set out and *murahbahs*, that is, preserved fruit, fig, grape, plum and cherry in syrup, were served, each in its own tiny glass dish.

It seemed to me that anyone ninety years old would be tired by now. We said we must go. Bidzula took our hands and urged us to stay.

"The afternoons are very long," she said, "and I enjoy company." So we sang a few more songs and finished another bottle of wine.

Bidzula may not have needed to rest, but by this time I did. No chance, however. Zina began the afternoon program by taking us to the day nursery where her sister worked. We found the children stacking their nap mats and putting their toys away before going home. They stopped long enough to come and see what Americans looked and sounded like, a treat, I suppose, like having a pair of kangaroos drop in.

Zina's other sister taught in a high school, so we stopped there for a quick tour. Her brother worked on a tea plantation just outside the city. He would be deeply offended, naturally, if we did not visit him, too, so we drove on and saw the slopes covered with sheared bushes and watched the mechanical tea picker lumbering up and down the rows pinching off the leaves with its iron fingertips.

By this time we had picked up quite a party and our single taxi had increased to a fleet of five. There must have been about twenty-five of us when we arrived back at Zina and David's for dinner. In minutes she had chicken soup with lemon and saffron on the table and, after that, red beans with herbs, cheese wrapped in mint leaves, leeks with nuts, rice and, to round out the meal, roast pork with a sauce of green grapes and coriander. It was midnight before we drank the last toast, and one of David's friends took us back to the sanitarium in his car.

In our room we found the electric tea kettle purring as usual and on the table a large tray covered with a linen cloth.

"Don't look," Helena said. "Push the table on the balcony and forget it."

My curiosity got the best of me. I lifted the cloth and found small filet of beef roasted on a skewer and sliced thin, corn bread, pickled cabbage, yogurt, a plate of greens, and a gelatin wreath studded with fruit. The balcony was scarcely large enough to hold it all.

Next morning breakfast appeared before we were dressed.

"We all worry," the maid said. "You have no appetite. You do not eat lunch. You do not eat dinner. You must take the baths to regain appetite and spirits."

She uncovered a plate of lean country ham, tiny hot fritters, fried cheese, crisp on the outside but melting within, eggplant baked with tomatoes and onions, and a pile of flat, crusty wheat bread we call *lavache*.

"I give up," I said to Helena and began on the fritters.

As we were going out we saw the director in the hall and after the customary inquiries about our comfort, he said, "Regretfully I must tell you the doctors advise you do not take the baths unless you can stay for the entire course of twenty-one days."

That, we said, was impossible.

"Then we must rely on our diet alone to restore your health, along of course with our good air. You visit your brother, too, which always makes one cheerful."

We certainly felt so that morning, for David and his

family and a dozen more friends called for us, and we drove
to Gelati along roads bordered with yellow azalea, the air
sweet with their fragrance and full of the hum of the bees
drinking their nectar. Near the top of the mountain we came
to the remains of the center of learning constructed by the
King we call David the Builder, about 1125.

He was a man of great size and strength, this King, and
he earned his name. The story says that when Gelati was
begun, David went himself to the quarry to select the corner-
stones.

After he made his choice, blocks six feet high by ten feet
wide weighing seven tons each, he reached down and
picked up the closest one and set it on his shoulder. "As long
as I'm here I might as well carry this piece home and save an
extra trip."

As the walls rose David worked with the masons until one
day he fell from the scaffold and broke his leg.

"I see," he said when his servants picked him up, "it takes
longer to learn how to lay stone than to rule a kingdom."

David lies buried beneath Gelati's great entrance arch.
On the flat stone covering his grave is carved: "This is my
eternal wish—let me lie where my people shall walk forever
on my heart." The letters are almost worn away.

Gelati stands in a sloping meadow, and we could walk
around and see it from various angles, above and below.
Like all ancient structures, it bears scars, but the assaults of
time and nature and man have not destroyed its beauty.
Although the academy is gone, the balance and symmetry
of the remaining buildings, two domed churches flanking
the cathedral, are undisturbed.

When we went inside, I felt as if I had opened a jewel box.

On the dull gold walls frescoes still glowed, saints, kings, queens, biblical scenes painted in colors that have kept their brilliance through the centuries.

After we looked our fill, we went out into the sun again and picnicked on the mountainside with blooming valleys spread below us.

We had another party that night at David's, and early the next morning, after eating the usual "small bite" and promising our friends at the sanitarium to return for a longer visit, we managed to get David, his family, and ourselves to the airport in time for the Tbilisi plane. When I tried to pay the taxi driver, who had spent two days driving us around, he refused.

"No, no," he said, looking shocked, "that was my small welcome-home present to you, and this," he took a basket of fruit from the trunk of the car, "is for farewell. To remember Kutaisi and Skaltupa."

"As if," Helena said when we were finally in flight, "anyone could ever, ever forget. My health is immeasurably improved. How about yours?"

CHAPTER SIX

All along Helena had worried that our trip to the village would give my stepmother and Irvandis' wife, who lived there, too much trouble.

"I hope they will not think of preparing any meal," Helena told my sisters. "Why don't we take a picnic with us?"

"Don't worry about it," Maro said.

"Something will be arranged," Eterre added.

When we arrived back in Tbilisi from Kutaisi, we found that Maro and my sister-in-law Eterre had already gone on ahead to the village.

"Tomorrow, Sunday," Leila said, "they expect the rest of us there."

"I wonder if they did take something for lunch with them?" Helena said. "We don't want to trouble Mother."

"I think we'll find enough there." Leila seemed uncon-
cerned.

"But we ought to be sure," Helena told me later. "I believe
I should buy a little bread and cheese and some fruit and a
bottle or two of wine, and we can picnic in a quiet corner
and not burden Mother."

"Good idea," I said, and with that we left it.

We had planned to go all together on the bus to Dushet,
which makes a stop in Kobiantkari on the way. But at eleven
o'clock when we assembled and were ready to set out for the
station, we found a car was waiting for us in front of the
hotel. It was not the small Moscovitz we had used oc-
casionally for sightseeing but a limousine so large and black
and gleaming that it looked like a monument carved from
a block of jet.

"Where does this come from?" I asked the man holding
the door for us.

"Director of Intourist Palavandishvily's own Lim with
his compliments and his driver. That's me. Levan." He shook
my hand.

"Nothing surpasses a Communist country," Helena said,
"when it comes to the luxuries of life."

"Perhaps so, but in any case a very kind gesture on the
director's part," I said. "He knows that the first time a man
goes back home, he likes to go in style."

In we piled, eight or nine of us, with Alexander's children
on the top layer and our parcels in the trunk. Levan took a
thoughtful look at the springs, checked each tire, got in,
started the engine and slowly, like a liner leaving the pier, the
Lim moved out of the drive and turned north.

At last I am on my way to my village.

Too fast the journey was. Every bend, every cluster of

houses we passed held a little piece of my life. Down this road I drove the turkeys to market; from the oven in the dooryard there a woman gave me hot corn bread on a cold winter day; here by the rock I sat to eat it.

Meantime, my brother Alexander was pointing out improvements along the way.

"Do you see the new bridge?"

"Yes." In the stream below I caught a trout two feet long, well, eighteen inches, anyway.

"And the café and gasoline station?"

"Yes." On the other side of the road, hidden in ferns, is a spring where the water gushes ice cold on the hottest day.

"Just ahead the road has been changed; the double curve is gone."

"Yes." The persimmon tree, too, but the walnut, thank God, still stands.

While I shuttled from past to present, we came to the crest of the mountain, turned off the main highway, and took the road through the woods and over a ridge, and there spread before me were the hillsides covered with cornelian cherries in golden bloom and below the roofs of my village caught the midday sun.

"Stop," I said to Levan. "Let me out here. You go on. I want to walk."

And so, after all, I came home as I left, on foot.

CHAPTER SEVEN

*H*ere is where my life started to begin when one day in a faraway August my third grandfather left our village below and followed a path of sunlight up, up, up the moutainside. Thinking to save time, he took a short cut over a steep ridge, and before he knew it he bumped into a cloud (for our mountains rise high enough to touch the sky), and all at once the trees, the rocky cliffs, the path, the very earth beneath his feet vanished from his sight.

"I am lost," he said to himself. "What shall I do?"

Now my third grandfather (he was really my great-uncle, but we had him for a spare grandfather) was a practical man, and he reasoned to himself, "If I stay here, I might stay forever. But if I keep walking, I must come to some place—; if the way leads up, perhaps to heaven; if it goes down, at least back to an inn where I can find bread and wine."

So on he went. When, later, the noon sun finally burned the clouds to ribbons of mist, he found himself in a mountain meadow that was all new to him.

Now my third grandfather's business was sheep, but his pleasure was his orchard. When he went out to buy fat-tailed rams or karacul kids, he often came home instead with his basket full of grafting twigs from some fine apricot or seeds of an extra sweet cherry, or, perhaps, under his arm, two or three wild plums he had dug up in the woods. That was my third grandfather for you.

On this August day, finding himself in a new place, he looked around with hunting eyes. A little below ran a fast stream, and above the stream stood a stone house, and next to the house grew a great tree full of golden pears. Picking the pears was a beautiful girl. . . . "The most beautiful girl," my third grandfather always said, when long after he told me the story, "and the finest pear tree that ever in my life I saw."

So he brushed his *cherkasska,* straightened his fur hat, smoothed his beard, and went down the hill calling out *"Gahmahr Jueba,"* our traditional greeting which means "Be you ever victorious."

The beautiful girl set down her basket and came to the gate.

"Gahgee Marjos. May you, too, be triumphant, Prince," she said. (My third grandfather had no title, of course, but that is the polite way to address any stranger.) "Come in and sit down and I will call my parents."

Immediately, her mother came from the house, and soon

her father, Elia, and her brother, Giorgi, came from the field, and they made my third grandfather welcome. For, in our country, we have a saying: "Praise God. From Him come all guests. God be praised."

They all sat down at the table under a grape arbor. The beautiful girl—her name was Eamdze, which means "violets in the sun"—brought them hot corn bread and white cheese, and a plate heaped high with fresh greens, cress and tarragon, and, of course, a great bowl of pears from the tree. As they ate, they told each other the story of their lives, and soon they were good friends.

It did not take my third grandfather long to see that Eamdze was as happy and good and wise as she was beautiful.

"What a fine wife she would make," he thought, "for one of the young men in my village—perhaps for my own nephew?"

But my third grandfather was a clever man and a careful man, and he spoke none of this aloud. Instead, he took a thoughtful look around the garden.

"I see you have no persimmons," he said to Elia.

"Alas, no, and it is my wife's favorite fruit, too," said Elia, "but we are too high in the mountains for persimmons to grow."

This led them to talk of trees and how to plant this and how to prune that, and they walked around the garden, and Elia insisted on giving his new friend slips and cuttings of his best plants. And so the day passed until after many thanks, good wishes and farewell, my third grandfather started back down the mountain toward home.

Once he reached the woods he pulled from its sheath the

dagger that hung from his belt, and as he went, he blazed trees to mark his way, for he knew before long he would be coming back. As soon as he reached Kobiantkari, he went to his favorite nephew, Vanno, who was just twenty-one.

"Vanno, I need your help. Will you go up the mountains with me?"

"With pleasure. When shall we start?"

"The day following the first frost."

A few weeks later, after the first October frost had turned the persimmons mellow, my third grandfather lined a willow basket with pine needles and filled it with perfect fruits, each one as round and burning bright as a little sun.

Vanno, true to his promise, came early to the door, shouldered the basket, and he and my third grandfather started up the mountain to Elia's house.

"A long, hard climb this is for me," said my third grandfather, who was as quick as a mountain goat. "Next time you must go alone."

"Next time?" said Vanno.

"Certainly. After my friend Elia presented me cuttings of all his choicest plants, how would it look if I give him in return only these few handfuls of persimmons?"

"No doubt you are right," Vanno said, hunching his load a little higher on his shoulders to ease his back. The old are wise, and to contradict them is very impolite.

They followed the trail to Elia's, delivered the persimmons and, of course, sat to rest and eat and talk before they started home. A few days later Vanno went up the mountain again with a basket of medlars, and next with a basket of russet pears, and after that with a basket of quince, and finally he went with no basket at all. Of course, the whole village saw this, for Kobiantkari was a very small place; the thirty-eight families who lived there were like a single household, and what happened to one concerned all.

True, it was a poor village without a post office, a mill, or a store. The church was a small building deep in the woods, where a priest came now and again for services.

The houses did not set along streets or around a square but were scattered helter-skelter over the mountainside, some a quarter mile apart, others within hailing distance, a few side by side, but all linked together by a narrow track more path than road.

No one had more than an acre, or at most two, of stony hillside for his own. All the good fields had to be rented from a prince who had lived so long in Moscow that his home and his language were both forgotten, and in fifty years he had never so much as touched his own ground with his own foot. The land meant nothing to him—only the money it would bring. This prince sent his relative, a man named Nestor, "Cruel Nestor" the village called him, to manage his estate and collect the share of the crop due him for using his land. After that was paid, little was left.

Of course, Kobiantkari had no hospital, no doctor, no school, no teacher. Worst of all, there was nobody, not one single person in the whole village that knew how to read or write. It made life hard.

When Cruel Nestor showed his account book and said this and that you owe, who could contradict him? If anyone bought or sold outside, he was at the trader's mercy. A message from a tax collector or a government inspector drove fear like a knife into every heart. When a man was conscripted for military service or left to find work beyond the mountains, it was like a death until he came back because, even if he found someone to write a letter home for him, who could read its message?

Yet no one in Kobiantkari ever wanted to leave and go to make another life in another place. Although the village might be poor and small, not even a pinpoint on the map, those who lived there thought it the center of the world. They would not have changed their mountainside for Tbilisi or Vladikavkaz, no, not even for St. Petersburg, where the Russian Czar sat on a golden throne in a marble palace and ate meat twice a day.

For Kobiantkari had meadows blue with primroses, thickets of blackberries, and whole hillsides of wild cornelian cherry trees, bright with golden flowers in the spring, hung with ruby fruit in summer. Through the village ran a stream called *Chwenes Tskale*, "Our Own," with water so delicious it was always said you could eat it as well as drink it. Best of all, those who lived in Kobiantkari had each other—neighbors, friends, relatives—to share sorrow and joy.

So when the day came, it was at New Year's, that Vanno announced he was going to marry Elia's daughter, Eamdze, in the spring, the whole village was delighted although not surprised.

"But wait," Vanno said as everyone drew around to shake his hand and wish him happiness, "you must know this is a very special bride I bring you. . . ."

"All brides are that," said Kalbatono Loucia, the oldest woman in the village. "I know without seeing her that she is, beyond words, good and beautiful."

"Yes, but more than that," Vanno said.

"She cooks well?" his friend Archil asked.

"Yes, but more than that . . ."

"She knows the herbs and how to heal?"

"More than that."

"She sews?"

"She knits?"

"She spins?"

"She sings?"

"She dances?"

"More than that! More than that . . ."

"Tell us."

Then, standing there as proud as any king, Vanno gave them the great news.

"She reads and writes."

CHAPTER EIGHT

Vanno and Eamdze, who became my parents, were married the next summer, and a year later I was born and grew in our house in the hillside. All I knew was to be loved and to be happy.

Every morning before dawn, while I still slept, my father harnessed Pretty One, our water buffalo, and went to plow the single acre we owned and the two we rented from the prince. When the sun rose high enough to touch our garden, my mother and I carried breakfast to him in the field. The three of us sat beside the hedgerow and ate potato soup and circles of hot bread filled with melted cheese. Pretty One rested in the shade and nibbled new grass. Sometimes my father would set me on her wide back. Then, holding so tight to her horns my fingers ached, I rode the length of the furrow.

Afterward, going home, my mother and I could hear my
father singing "Oravella":

> My plow cuts the furrow deep,
> My buffalo does not sleep.
> Pull, Pretty One, pull.

As we walked we joined in, our voices answering his:

> Whose plow cuts the furrow deep?
> Whose buffalo does not sleep?
> Our Pretty One, ours.

Whenever my father found a day's work in Dushet, the
next town, he left me in charge of the house.

"Help your mother," he always said, the last thing as he
went out the gate.

And I did. I brought sticks for the fire and piled them
neatly. I swept the yard with a broom made of twigs. I fed
our dog, Murka, and her puppy, Basar. I gave fresh corn
nubbins to our golden colt, Challa. When my mother took our
washing to the stream below our house, I carried one side
of the basket. While she scrubbed our clothes on the rocks,
I waded in the pools at the water's edge and with pebble
dams made lakes to float leaf boats until it was time to carry
the basket home again.

In a clearing back of our house we had a vegetable garden,
and I helped my mother plant cucumbers, gogra, a pumpkin
sweet as honey, beans, and eggplant.

Beyond our gate was God's garden—not set in neat rows
like ours—but spreading its bounty through hedgerows,
woods, and fields, and all free for the taking. There, in spring,
my mother and I hunted for the first wild greens—sorrel and

cress, peppery purslane, and the seeds of the herb we call "the fragrance that came from faraway."

When summer came, we took our baskets and gathered wild apples and quince, sour plums to make into sauce, green walnuts for jelly and, what I liked best, the golden tassels of the jonjoli tree for pickling.

In the fall my mother and I searched in the darkest corners of the woods for those special mushrooms that stand in mourning circles where old apple trees have died.

Sometimes we made a holiday and went to visit our nearest neighbor, my mother's friend Daro, who lived on the opposite hillside. Although we could see her house from our dooryard, it was a long journey to go there. First, we crossed a rushing stream, stepping from one slippery stone to another; then we climbed up the steep bank and followed a narrow path through a thicket, where once we saw a snake as thick and black as rope. After that we came to a road, and there we had to pass two fierce dogs who guarded the prince's vineyard. But whenever I began to feel afraid, my mother's hand always found mine, and somehow the danger passed.

The summer I was four my mother did not walk in the woods with me any more, nor did we go to the field. Daro came and took our clothes to wash. My father carried his breakfast with him in the morning; at night, when his work was done, he and I brought water from the stream.

During the long hot afternoons of that July and August my mother sat on the bench under our great beech tree. I played on the ground with a toy cart my father had made me. As she sewed and mended she recited to me parts of our country's great poem, "The Man in the Panther's Skin," which she knew by heart.

I did not understand what it meant, but I liked to hear her say the words. She told me old stories—about the Narts, the great-headed giants who lived peacefully together on earth before men were created and wars began, about St. Giorgi on his white horse who killed all the dragons, about Amirani who snatched fire from heaven and made the gods so angry they chained him to a rock on our highest mountain.

"And is he still there?" I asked.

"Still there," my mother said, "but though men have forgotten Amirani, his little dog has stayed by his side licking at the chains for a thousand thousand years, and one day he will free him."

"Would Basar stay with me, if I was on the mountainside a thousand years?"

"If you had always been good to them, I think Basar would, and Murka, too."

They were sleeping in the shade, but, hearing their names, Basar flopped his tail and Murka opened her clever eyes and dozed again.

September came, and when the harvest was over, my father told me one morning that he was going to Muhkran to get my Aunt Salome and bring her to our house.

"Can I go with you?" I said.

"Not this time. You must keep watch here until I come home, probably late tonight. Stay close so you can help your mother."

I was proud and called Murka and Basar and walked them up and down until they grew tired and sat down in the coolest place they could find. I went to the door and called my mother to come outside and tell me stories.

"Not now," she said. "Not now." She was lying on the *tahkte*. "You play with your toys and stay close by."

I went into the yard, tried to spin the top my father had carved for me, but the string tangled. I made some carts out of walnut shells and pushed them along a rack until I grew tired of that. Then for a while I was Amirani on the mountainside, but Murka showed she would rather sleep than be my faithful dog and Basar had more interest in chasing his own tail than in licking away my chains.

So I turned into St. Giorgi with a stick for my white horse and Basar for my dog, and we chased the dragons around the yard until we caught them, every one. But we did not kill any, because the oldest dragon promised to take his family and go away and live in the woods and never come out again. All the people in our village, and in Dushet, too, were proud of me and they made a party and sang *Mhraval Jahmee Eh*—"May You Live Through All Time."

I was going to sing the answer—"Thank you, Thank you" —as my father did when his friends drank a toast to him, but Basar began to paw at a stone and I went to see why.

A great horned beetle crawled out, snapping its pinchers at me. I ran to our door and told my mother how fierce it looked.

"Perhaps the beetle thinks the same of you," my mother said. She was still lying down.

"I will hit it with a stone before it bites me."

"No, if you don't hurt the beetle, it won't hurt you. You go your way, let the beetle go his. The world is large enough for you both."

I tiptoed back. The beetle was still there, but he looked a little more friendly.

"Would you like a blackberry?" I rolled one near his mouth. I guess he wasn't very hungry.

Basar put his nose close to the beetle.

"Leave him alone," I said, "if you don't hurt him, he won't hurt you. The world is big enough for you both."

Basar sat back on his haunches, and we watched the beetle until he finally crawled away and disappeared in a forest of grass. Basar and I were digging under the stone to see what was in a beetle's house when I heard my mother cry out. I looked up. She was standing in the doorway.

"You must go to Daro. Now! Tell her I need her."

"You will come with me."

"No."

"But I can't go alone."

"Yes, you can."

I came to the porch and took her hand. "You come, too."

"No. This time you must go alone, and as quickly as you can. Say to her, 'My mother needs you.'"

I went out to the gate and then I came back. "I forget the way."

My mother wiped her face. "You will remember. Hurry."

I went close to her and whispered, "I'm afraid."

"No, you are a man. You are brave. You are not afraid."

"I'll be alone."

"Not really. I'll stand here at the door, and whenever you turn around you can see me."

"Not from the thicket!"

"No, but even there you will know I am here."

"If I fall in the stream?"

"You will get wet . . . and dry again in the sun."

"The snake . . ."

"Make a noise and no snake will come near you."

"The dogs by the vineyard?"

"Here is bread. Break it in half as you go near and throw each of the dogs a piece."

I put the bread inside my blouse.

"Hurry!" my mother said.

I went out the gate and down the path that led to the stream. The water looked very black, and I stepped out to the first stone, and the second, and the third. There I froze. I could go neither forward nor backward. The water lapped at my feet, whirled around, caught a leaf and sucked it into a dark pool. Slowly, slowly, without moving my feet I turned my head. My mother still stood on the porch, and she waved her hand.

I took a deep breath and a big step and reached the next stone and the next until I was close enough to the far side to jump to the pebbled beach.

Was my mother still watching? Yes. I started up the bank. I was almost to the top when I slipped and slid all the way down again. My legs were scratched, one knee was bleeding, and my bread was gone. I wanted to cry, but I knew my mother would be waiting. I washed my cuts in the water, found my bread, and climbed the bank again. When I reached the top, I could see our house and my mother still there. I waved and she waved back. I went on.

I began to sing a song, not because I felt happy, but to frighten the snakes. For in the thicket I knew hundreds and hundreds waited, slipping, sliding, their forked tongues darting. A curled root, a rustling in the leaves, a shifting shadow, each in turn stopped my heart until finally I had no more breath to sing. Then I began to run—to run through briers that caught my clothes and tore my hands and tried every way to hold me there. But at last I broke free and came to the top of the hill.

I looked back. My mother was gone. I was alone. Then I saw a flash of white. She *was* there! She was waving her veil. I went on.

The vineyard dogs had heard me crashing through the thicket, and they began to bark. They were big dogs with sharp teeth and long tongues. If only I were a Nart and I could step over them with giant legs; if only I were St. Giorgi—or his white horse; if only I were a dragon, even the smallest dragon; if only I were Amirani with fire in my hand; if only—but I was nobody—nobody at all.

The dogs were running toward me. Frightened, I threw the bread too soon. They took it at one gulp and raced at me. If I ran, they would surely catch me, maybe eat me up and I couldn't help my mother. I stopped still, my back against the fence.

"Be quiet," I said in my loudest voice. "Go home!"

Would they snap off my fingers and gulp them down, sink their teeth into my arms, my legs? The big dog stopped barking and watched me. The smaller one came close, sniffing me, his lips curled.

"Go home!" I said again. "The world is big enough for us both."

The big dog scratched his ear and yawned, and after a few minutes he turned around and trotted home. The little dog, seeing this, went after him, and they both lay down by their gate.

All at once the road was mine. I walked along it, proud, to Daro's house and gave her my mother's message. What she said, how and when I went back home, I have forgotten.

The next day my father showed me my new brother David. I was not much interested in him. He was only a baby, and I had grown to be a man.

CHAPTER NINE

*N*ow I wandered everywhere. The fields, the river, the woods, the whole world and all that was in it belonged to me.

When we took breakfast to my father in the field, it was I who carried the basket while my mother held David. Four we were, sitting in the hedgerow with the grey stone for our table. When our meal was over and my mother started back home with David, I stayed to help my father. Together we sang "Oravella," as we followed the plow, our voices floating out over the green fields to meet my mother's answering notes.

After our day's work was done, my father set me high on Pretty One's back. Holding fast to her horns, I rode her through the village to the lake for her evening bath. All water buffalo of course love the water that names them, but none more than Pretty. She was, I often thought, more than half fish. Once into the lake, she rolled and swam and sloshed and wallowed, and no matter how I coaxed, "Come out, Pretty One, come out," there she stayed until the very marrow of her bones was wet. Only then, sleek and dark and round as an eggplant, her skin rippling over her bones, would she be ready to go home with me.

On dark nights our house was hard to see, for it was small, one room built into the hillside. The floor was pounded earth. There were no windows; the only light came through a single door. The fireplace in the center of the room had no chimney —just a hole in the roof to let the smoke out—when the wind blew right. Against the whole length of the back wall was our *tahkte,* a low wide shelf we used by day for a table, and at night, covered with quilts, as our bed.

For years my father dreamed of building a new house, a fine house, a house that stood free of the hill, a house with four proud straight standing walls. Often and often he drew his plan on the floor with a pointed stick.

"Here will be the corners," he would tell my mother and me. "Here to this side a stone fireplace with a wide chimney that laughs at the wind, here, a door, here, a partition to make two rooms, here—but when will it ever be—?"

"Someday," my mother always said, "someday."

But when? In our village a man traded with his neighbors for almost everything he needed: grain for barley, milk for cheese, a day's work plowing for a day's work threshing, your horse two days for my buffalo four, I mend your wagon, you carve me a saddle. We lived with neither coins nor written-down numbers, and each man kept his own accounts in his own heart.

But building a house was different. That took cash—at least forty rubles—a fortune. In his whole life, working every day more hours than the sun, my father had saved only eleven rubles. Two of these he lent to help his friend Archil buy a horse, and another he had to give to the priest for prayers when my mother's mother died the year I was born. Eight rubles were left.

My father had golden hands, and he could do anything that came his way—weave willow baskets fine enough to hold flour, make wheels for buffalo carts, braid rope—but there was no one in Kobiantkari rich enough to pay him in cash. For that he had to go to Dushet, a town two miles away. Even there, work was scarce. My father thought himself lucky to be hired one or two days in a week. Whenever he did bring home a day's wages, we counted out the coins on the table after supper—seven, eight, nine, maybe ten showre pieces were the most he could earn, and it took one hundred showre to make one ruble. Some cash, too, we had to spend now and then, one showre for salt, another for tea, half a showre for a spool of thread. Nevertheless, two or three we managed always to save, and my father let me drop them into an earthen jar where we kept the new house money.

Now, my mother had, when she married, a golden chain from her godmother. She kept it wrapped in a silk handkerchief in a little wooden box my father made for her. Often she took the chain out and polished the links carefully, and she let me hold it and carefully trace the carved design with my fingertip. On great holidays, when she wore her good dress and her best head veil, she looped the chain around her neck.

One morning after my father had gone to Dushet to work I was gathering wood when I heard a great clanging and banging beyond the hill. I knew what it meant, and I ran to tell my mother.

"The Syrians are coming."

Once or twice a year these peddlers, their donkeys piled high with copperware, came rattling through our village. They mended old pots or traded them for new ones, and they bought and sold metal, too.

The Syrian's donkeys were old friends of mine. I hurried to bring water from the brook and cut some bunches of new grass to be ready for their arrival. While I fed them and brushed their ragged coats, the Syrians talked as best they could to my mother. To hear them swallow the words and twist the sentences made me laugh. But not out loud. My mother had forbidden me ever to do that—even when a Russian tried to speak our language.

"Remember," she said, "they are guests and must be respected."

Patiently my mother tried to tell the Syrians she could buy nothing that day.

They would not hear.

"Water jug?" the oldest man said.

"No."

"Good, good." One of the younger men thumped the side of the piece to prove it.

"No."

"Tray?" The bright circle caught my mother's face and for a moment held it, like an icon.

"No, perhaps another day."

The Syrians began to repack their goods, and I gave each donkey one farewell munch of grass.

"If I cannot sell, then I must buy," the old man said. "Surely you have a broken scissors, a worn knife, perhaps an old coin, an ornament turned up in the field. I buy anything. Anything. A crooked nail or a king's crown."

My mother went into the house and in a minute she was out again with something in her hand.

"Will you buy this?" she said. She held out her golden chain.

The old man looked at it a long time and then passed it to the younger ones, and they talked in their own language.

"Two rubles," he said finally.

"Six," my mother said.

"Three!"

"No," my mother said.

"Four!"

My mother shook her head. "Six!" (I had never seen her bargain before.)

At last the Syrian reached under his coat and brought out a leather bag, and as sadly as if he were breaking pieces off his own heart he counted one—two—three—four—five—six silver rubles into my mother's hand.

After the Syrians were gone my mother and I went into the house. She folded the silk handkerchief very flat and laid it in the wooden box and set the box back in its usual place on the shelf.

Her eyes were full of tears, but she was smiling.

"We will surprise your father."

She let me drop the coins into the pot. Clink, clink, clink, clink, clink, clink. What a rich sound they made as they fell.

That very night we did surprise my father and he us, for he came home full of good news. His friend Archil paid back the two rubles he borrowed long before to buy the horse.

Now our pot held sixteen silver rubles and nearly three more in showre pieces. Nineteen rubles in all.

My father had more to tell us. A rich man was buying an orchard beyond Dushet, and he would pay my father in cash to set a fence around the whole property.

"I will earn at least half a ruble a week and when spring comes and the days are longer, maybe even a ruble."

"I will come, too," I said. "I will help."

My father looked doubtful. "You had better stay home," he said. "To make fences is the hardest work in the world— so hard that it makes one think that perhaps God does not like men to be so jealous of their own."

I coaxed and coaxed until finally my father said, "All right, come with me tomorrow." Then you will see and be satisfied to stay home."

My father was right. To watch men make fences, at least the kind of fences we had in Georgia, must have made God sad and the devil laugh out loud.

First, my father and I had to dig holes—three feet deep, four feet apart up hill and down, between stones and through thickets. My bones ached when we went home that night, but I was too proud to admit it. The next day and the next and the next I went with my father.

After the holes were all dug we went to the woods and cut young trees, trimmed off the branches, sharpened both ends, set one in each hole, put the dirt back and tramped it solid. Nothing, I thought, could be harder than that, but I was wrong.

When the stakes were all in, we went to a woods where a special bush grew—a bush with thorns three inches long. We cut branches, tramped them into tight bunches and tied them with lengths of wild vine. Then we carried these bundles to the field and pushed them down on the sharp poles until they reached shoulder height. My hands and feet were like raw meat that night, and my mother rubbed them with herbs mixed in oil.

"You see now," my father said, "why you cannot help me. Later, when you are older . . ."

But next day I wrapped my feet in some rags before I put on my shoes, and I went again. Before too many days I knew how to cut and tramp and tie and carry and stack the thorn bushes with only enough stabs to keep me respectful.

At the end of the week my father and I had earned a whole ruble to drop in the crock. When that fence was finally finished and we counted out our coins, we had thirty-four rubles.

"Is it enough?" I asked my father.

"To begin our house? Yes. Now I will send word to your Uncle Giorgi. He promised he would help us when we were ready."

Two days later Dzea Giorgi came down the mountain, his stone hammer and chisels in a pack on his back, his dog Juliko at his heels.

Our Murka traded some throat growls and sneery lips with Juliko, but when Dzea Giorgi said softly, "Come, come be friends," tails began to wag, and off they went together to treat each other to laps of water from the brook. All animals understood Dzea Giorgi and obliged him the best they could, and no wonder, for he did the same by them.

Next morning my father marked out the plan on the ground, and Dzea Giorgi began to dress the stones we had been carrying ever since I could remember, one by one from the fields. Clink. Clink. With two hammer strokes he squared off a corner; clank, the side was straight, he positioned his chisel; clank again, and the stone split into two equal parts.

In a trough made from a hollowed log my father and I mixed the mortar—sand and lime and water—and to bind it fast all the golden hair we had curried from Challa since he was a colt.

Day by day, like a miracle, the walls grew up and up—past my ankles, past my knees, past my belt, almost to my chin. . . .

"Stop," my father said then. "Don't lay any more stone until I come back."

He harnessed Pretty One to our cart and started toward Dushet.

CHAPTER TEN

"Well, while we wait, why don't we make a holiday for ourselves?" Uncle Giorgi asked me.

"Yes, yes, Dzea," I said. To walk with him was to see the world with new eyes.

My mother put a loaf of brown bread freshly baked in the outdoor oven and a round ball of cheese in a shoulder basket for us, and off we went to the woods, Dzea walking ahead as silently as a feather floats, I following after, until we came to a fast brook. He stopped.

"Shall we catch trout?" he asked me.

"We have no hook, no line."

"We need none. Watch."

He knelt on the bank. In the water near some rocks he dipped one hand, then the other; without a ripple, like two fish, they moved toward each other, met beneath the stone, and three fish came to the surface—the middle one a speckled trout. Gently, Uncle Giorgi let him slip back into the water.

"Let me find one," I said.

Uncle Giorgi showed me how to hold my hands and bring them closer, closer, but the first trout had warned all the others, and I had no luck.

We followed the brook on up the mountain. Suddenly, Uncle Giorgi stopped and sniffed the air. I did, too.

"What passed by here?"

"I don't know," I said.

"Deer walking in the water to hide their track."

He drew another deep breath. "What else is near?"

I wrinkled my nose like Basar scenting a rabbit.

"Dead leaves?"

"What else?"

"Dead leaves and black dirt . . ."

"And growing in them mushrooms for our lunch. Come, let's look."

Sure enough, under a beech we found enough of the orange ones we call fox tails to fill my cap.

Uncle Giorgi had his mason's hammer in his belt, and now and then he stopped, tapped a rock, and listened to its ring. He loved stones; to him their form and color and texture were as beautiful as flowers. He could turn a boulder and say which way it would cleave; he always knew somehow what color lay hidden beneath the weathered surface scale.

We walked on, stopping to gather filberts, to listen to the jays talking, to watch the kites circling far above us. Dzea showed me where the wild pigs had hunted acorns beneath an oak and a little farther on a bear's resting place in a thicket.

We came to a yellow stream; the water was warm and smelled of rotten eggs.

"It comes from a sulphur spring above," Dzea said. "Let us follow it. We may see something."

In a little way the stream fell over a steep cliff. We crept to the edge and looked down. There, beside the pool, lapping the rocks were three mountain sheep, their noses and horns and lips gilded like icons from the sulphur. One scented us, squeaked a warning, and off they went in an arc that carried them out of sight.

"Why do they eat sulphur?"

"I think it is medicine for them," Dzea said. "Often I have seen old ones near sulphur springs."

We gathered a few golden pebbles from the river and a bouquet of gentians for my mother. By sunset we were home. My father was still gone. It was almost dark before the creak of his wagon wheels brought us all to the door.

"Come out!" my father called before he turned into the yard. "Come out and see!"

The back of the cart held a thousand stars shining as brightly as the ones in the sky above.

"What is it?" my mother said, going close.

"Windows. Glass windows for our new house. One for each well."

Next morning the windows were set in place, and the walls grew around them with stones laid up in Uncle Giorgi's best pattern—a row slanted left, then one to the right, back and forth.

When the roof beams were raised, my father sent me to ask all the neighbors to a party. Beneath our great beech tree the table was set. On it were plates of greens, cress, tarragon, salt cheese to tuck into circles of flat white bread. My mother had chicken roasted flat between two earthen plates and hot golden corn bread and boiled nettles in nut sauce and eggplant baked with tomatoes. Our neighbors could hardly eat for looking at our new house.

"Two rooms!"

"A fireplace . . . with no smoke. Surely the Czarina herself has no finer place to cook for her family."

"And the proof of it is this delicious dinner Kalbatono Eamdze has made for us," said my father's friend Archil, putting another spoonful of sour-plum sauce on his chicken.

The whole warm afternoon we sat around the table eating and singing. There were toasts to my father and my mother, to David, to me, to our happy life in our new house. My father and I answered their good wishes, and I, all by myself, sang the proper thanks without missing a note—except a few in the middle and one or two at the beginning and the end.

When it grew dark, my father built a fire and roasted sticks of *m'tswade*, broiled lamb. We had more toasts. My father drank to Uncle Giorgi and told how he laid the stone. We all sang "*Mhraval Jahmee Eh*" to him, and he had me help him sing his thanks.

David and the other babies fell asleep and were carried in to the *tahkte*, but the rest of us sat outdoors, talking, telling stories, and finally Archil touched the strings of his *chonguri*, and we danced and the stars in the sky danced with us.

When at last our party was over and our guests were starting home, Kalbatano Lucia, the oldest lady in our village, began to worry about our windows.

"Perhaps on second thought you should close them up," she said to my mother. "A stranger might look into your house. And if the glass breaks, it will cut your children to pieces. What use, after all, are such openings?"

"To see outside," my mother said.

"Why? The trees, the stones, the mountains, they stay the same year in and year out and need no watching. In my day, a door was enough for anybody, but now . . ."

"It will give more light within," said my father politely.

She shook her head. "Young people are never satisfied." Soon holes in the walls will not be enough but you will have holes in the roof and holes in the floor, too."

Everyone else was proud. To think Kobiantkari had a house with four glass windows. *That* was something to mention when they visited friends in the next village.

Beside our door my mother planted roses to climb to the roof, and at the windows she hung curtains of soft red wool cloth from her own spinning. Now when I brought Pretty One home at dusk I could see from far away our lights shining from our windows and our smoke rising from our chimney. Inside all was warm and bright and fragrant from the bunches of lemon verbena my mother always hung to dry near the fireplace. The candle threw a golden circle on the table, the hearth was swept clean, and in the pot something bubbled.

After we ate our dinner my mother put David to bed singing softly to him until he fell asleep. Then we three sat on by the fire.

My mother wanted to teach me and my father, too, how

to read and write. We had no book, no pencil, and no paper, but my father sanded a straight pine board on both sides, rounding the corners neatly, and for markers he whittled thin sticks to a point and charred one end in the fire.

"It is as good, it is better than any slate," my mother said. "See, I make *a* and after you learn that, I can brsuh it away —like this—and show you *b*."

Almost every night we drew our letters—*a* we learned, and *b*, and then *g*, which in our alphabet comes third.

"*G* is your letter," my mother said.

G looked like a fish swimming toward me. I made so many *G*'s I wore out our marking stick, and my father had to cut and char another.

After *G* came *D* shaped like a flower with a stem and a leaf. *D* was our David's letter. I drew a whole garden of *D*'s on the board.

At *E* my father, who could shoe a horse, make a barrel, or split a tree in half with one stroke, gave up.

"There is a time to learn everything," he said, "and the time for letters is past. For me. Not for you."

I kept on through *i* and *k* and *l*, but there the lessons stopped, and so did our happy life.

My mother carried another child. One day she was smiling at me and calling my name; the next she and my newborn sister were dead.

$\mathcal{M}$y father's oldest sister, my Aunt Salome, lived in Muhkran twenty miles away. She was a widow. In the very first year of her marriage her husband, his brother, and the brother's wife all died of typhus. Of the whole family, left only were Salome and her husband's nephew, Alexander. Aunt Salome made Alexander her own child.

When my mother died, my aunt told my father she would take me and our David home to Muhkran to live with her and Sandro, who then was about eleven.

"No," my father said, "I will keep them here with me."

Although he tried the best he could and our neighbors helped us, too, I guess my father soon saw he could not manage alone. One morning he wakened me so early the stars were still bright.

"Wash yourself and put on a clean blouse."

"Where are we going?"

"To Muhkran. To Aunt Salome."

"Are we going to ride Challa?"

"No. Three of us and the basket are too heavy for him."

As soon as I made ready, I helped my father dress David. While we ate some bread and a bowl of water-buffalo milk, my father put all our clothes into a basket. When I saw him pack my red blouse, I knew we were going to stay in Muhkran a long time, surely until Easter, maybe forever.

When we were all ready to go David, usually so good-natured, began to cry. My father tried to quiet him, but he only screamed louder. I knew why. He wanted his toy horse. I looked under the *tahkte* and outdoors in the garden, and finally I found it in the deep grass and brought it to him. Then he stopped crying.

"Can he take it with him?" I asked my father.

"Yes. Do you want your cart and your top?"

"No," I said, "I would rather they wait for me here in our house."

My father fed Basar and Murka. "Guard the house," he told them.

They sat and watched us with longing eyes. I put my head against Murka. She licked my face. "Guard the house," I said. I knelt down and petted Basar. "Guard the house."

I went out and closed our gate behind me.

My father had David on one shoulder, the basket on the other. I walked beside him, and I turned and looked back as often as I could. First Basar disappeared, then the roses growing over our door and, at last, all that was left was our smoke rising from our chimney. Then we started down the other side of the mountain, and I could see no more.

As we walked along, my father explained why he was taking us to my aunt's to live.

"In your aunt's house you will have regular meals—with fresh bread to eat—"

"I like dry bread better," I said.

"Soon it will be winter and I must find work in Dushet, and I would be gone all day."

"I would wait for you," I said, "and keep the fire going."

"But somebody must watch David."

"I could do that, too," I said. "I would never let him go near the fire or wander into the woods. I would take him walking. I could even carry him if he got tired."

"Yes, but you must both have food—"

"I remember where to find berries and nuts and pears, too."

"And your clothes washed."

"I could do that, too."

"I know you could," my father said, "but for a little while you and David will be better with your aunt. And you will be good and obedient, I know, and help her all you can."

When in late afternoon we came to my aunt's house, we were all tired, David, especially, and my aunt gave him bread and milk and took him away to bed.

Sandro was glad to see me, and he showed me the *tahkte* where we would sleep. He gave me his new sling stone to try, and when I tired of that he tossed knucklebones with me and let me win every game until Aunt Salome called us to our supper.

New bread fresh from the oven was on the table, and potatoes fried crisp and brown on the outside, and new green beans from the garden cooked with eggs, a feast.

But I had no appetite.

"You must eat," my father said.

Not to hurt my aunt's feeling I put some bread in my mouth, but my throat seemed too small to swallow even a crumb. The potatoes, the beans, the eggs, everything had lost its taste, but I took one bite and then another.

Aunt Salome talked; my father answered; Sandro spoke; I said yes and no and thank you; our voices sounded like echoes.

When our meal was finally over, my father said he must start back to Kobiantkari.

"It is so late and you are tired," Aunt Salome said. "You will not be home until long after midnight."

"There is a moon," my father said.

"Stay tonight, Vanno," Aunt Salome said, "and go in the morning."

"No, tomorrow early I have a job in Dushet—fitting a wheel."

He put on his coat and kissed us, each one, me the last, and he told me again to help Aunt Salome and take care of David. Then he was gone.

"I'll play you *chelekahobah*," Sandro said. He cut the sticks, one to throw into the air, the other to strike it with. I had no heart for the game.

So we sat on the ground, and Sandro told me all the things we would do together in the days to come.

"Tomorrow," he said, "it is my turn to take the village sheep to the upper meadow to graze. I earn one showre.

You'll come with me? We'll be partners . . . and divide the money."

That was a great honor. Sandro was almost twelve, and I was not yet six. Any boy in the village would be proud to be partners with him, to have such a responsibility, to earn money.

"And we will take the dogs with us," he said, "in case wolves come."

I thought of my Murka and my good Basar waiting, waiting for me by the gate.

"We'll take bread," Sandro said, "and perhaps Mamedah, for a treat, will give us sausage and we can make a fire like hunters and roast it. You will like that?"

"Yes."

"And there is a stream and just maybe I can catch a fish— a barbel or a carp—if you want me to?"

"Yes."

"And we can broil our fish over the fire. Would you like that?"

"Yes."

"In the stream is a pool where we can wade and still watch the sheep, too. And I know a hollow tree where a fox comes. Do you want to see a fox?"

"Yes."

Sandro finally fell asleep, but I could not. The pillow, the blanket, the sound of the house were strange; even the air seemed too solid to breathe.

In the morning Aunt Salome gave us our bread and cheese and a piece of sausage, too, to take with us, and we collected all the sheep in the village and four of the best herding dogs and drove them toward the mountain. When we came to the fork where the road divided, I stopped.

"I'm not going with you," I told Sandro. "I'm going home to Kobiantkari."

"Does Aunt Salome know?"

I shook my head. "You tell her tonight."

Sandro did everything he could to discourage me.

"You've never come all by yourself, you don't know the way."

"Yes, I do. I remember from yesterday."

"You might meet a wolf."

I broke a branch from a tree. "I'll drive him away."

"There might be ten wolves."

"Not in daytime."

"But you can't get home until night."

"I'll run part way and be there before dark."

He tried to dissuade me, but there was nothing he could do. He had the sheep to watch, and he could neither come with me nor go back and tell Mamedah.

Finally, when he saw I was determined, he gave me all the cheese and sausage and most of the bread.

"I will come again," I said, ". . . for a visit. We can catch the fish then, and see your fox, too, and play knucklebones." I started off and then I turned back. "I would rather be your partner than anybody's, Sandro, if I could stay. Good-bye. Be victorious."

"Be you, too, victorious," Sandro said. "If you should meet a wolf, sing. Loud. They are afraid of music, or so I heard."

The way back seemed much longer than when my father and David and I walked together.

It was slower, too. Every time I heard the creaking wooden wheels of a buffalo cart, I hid in the woods and waited until it passed, for I did not want anyone from Muhkran or from Kobiantkari to see me.

As I walked I wondered what my father would say. I had not thought of that before.

It was almost dark when I came over the last hill and I could see our house. No smoke rose from the chimney, no light shone from the windows, but Murka and Basar heard my step and ran out, barking, until they saw it was not a stranger but me. Basar jumped and licked my face, and Murka took my hand in her great mouth and pulled me into the dooryard.

The house was silent, my father gone.

I lay down on my *tahkte* with my head on my own pillow, my own blanket over me. Basar jumped up beside me and tucked his head under my arm. Murka curled up at my feet. I heard the creak-creak-creak of our roof beam settling itself for the night, the whish-whish-whish of our rose branches against the window, the whoo-whoo-whoo of the owl who lived in our woods. With Basar and Murka close beside me, I fell asleep.

CHAPTER TWELVE

When I woke up in the morning, I could hear my father chopping wood outside. Before I had dressed myself he came in carrying logs. I waited for him to scold me.

"Come to breakfast," was all he said. "You must be hungry."

After we ate he told me to go to the pasture and catch Challa. That was easy, for as soon as he heard my whistle he came nuzzling for the piece of bread he knew I always brought him.

When I rode him into the yard, my father said, "Now you must go back to Muhkran; your Aunt Salome will be very worried about you."

"I told Sandro to tell her I went home and to say thank you."

"Do you think that is good manners? To ask another person to pay your compliments?"

"No," I said.

"Then go to Muhkran. Tell her for yourself that you are sorry you went away without a word and thank her."

"Do I have to stay?"

"No. Let Challa rest three hours. Then you can ride back here."

Off I went, and I came home again that night—and sometimes in the days that followed I was almost sorry I had.

At first it seemed my mother was everywhere. Outdoors, I thought I heard her call me; indoors, her dress rustled, her song echoed. Wherever I went I saw mothers—but never mine—sheep nursed their lambs, birds flew to the little ones in the nests, even the fox sheltered her cubs in a hollow tree. When I slept, it was to dream it was all a dream, and each morning I woke to lose my mother all over again.

Then, as the days and weeks and months passed, she vanished, and that was worse. Try as I would, I could not remember the sound of her voice, the touch of her hand, no not even her face—all, all were gone.

"You must be good and help your father and keep him in the best heart you can," Aunt Salome told me whenever I went to visit her.

I tried. I brought water from the well, and I went to the woods and gathered up sticks and cones for the fire. I swept the floor as I had seen my mother do and pulled the blankets as straight as I could on our beds, but the house did not look the same. Maybe a bouquet? I picked flowers, tied them in a bunch, and set them in three twigs to hold them straight. My father hardly noticed what I did. He lost interest in life. Always, always, he was good to me, but I guess part of him died with my mother. Often I wished he would talk to me about her, but I saw he could not. Only once so long as he lived did I ever hear him speak her name.

He lent our land and Pretty One to his friend Archil, and found work making wagon wheels in Dushet. Sometimes I went with him and helped, but when he had to go to another village farther away for a day or two, I stayed at home. Then Murka and Basar and I went where we would—into the forest or high, high up the mountains or along the road as far as the next village. There was no one to care if I came early or came late or came not at all.

Once in a month or perhaps twice, if the weather was good, I walked to Muhkran to see David. While I was there, Aunt Salome washed my clothes and washed me, too, and fed me as many meals as I would eat.

Aunt Salome's living came from a vineyard. On a small three-cornered piece of ground, bordered on one side by a little brook and on the other by a band of trees that tempered the wind, she raised the finest white grapes in the district. Of course, Sandro helped her and David, too, as he grew older, and whenever I went to Muhkran I worked with them. In late winter we pruned the vines back to one gnarled stalk that sprang to leaf again with the first spring rains. After that we trimmed all the extra sprouts away. Then it was time for Sandro and me to go to the woods and cut snelle, long thin new growth saplings, for trellises. Between times we chopped weeds with our hoes, for it was Mamedah's pride to have her vineyard floor a black velvet carpet with no spot of green anywhere on it.

In September, I always went to Muhkran when the grapes

were ripe. My father wove willow baskets with arm loops so Sandro and I could wear them on our backs and keep both hands free. For as we snapped the stems we lifted the heavy bunches, each pale green grape dusted with golden bloom, from the vine. When our basket was full, we took it to the arbor where Aunt Salome made wine.

When the grapes were pressed, Sandro and I had to go down and clean the quevre. This great earthen wine vat as big as a room was buried in the ground beneath the arbor. Once inside, all we could see was a tiny circle of sky at the opening. When we spoke, our voices sounded like church bells. We scrubbed the sides of the quevre with twig brushes and washed it clean and rinsed it three times, taking turns bailing the water out.

"Once more," Aunt Salome always said, "just to make sure."

More pails of water from the well, more sloshing. At last out we came into the sunshine and in went the wine; the earthen cover was put on and sealed tight with mud, a flagstone was set over it, then a sifting of earth, and the wine was left to itself for a year.

From the last, the sweetest picking of grapes, Mamedah made her famous *chuchkella*, for no one in the village would have considered himself born or married if Aunt Salome's *chuchkella* had not been served at his christening party or set on his wedding table. First, Sandro and I cracked nuts, filberts, whole, or walnuts in the perfect halves that Mamedah needed. To save her the trouble of sorting we ate the broken pieces.

At night as we sat around the fire we strung the nut meats tightly on a heavy thread about a hand span long and finished with a loop at the top. Next Mamedah simmered grape juice and white flour to a thick syrup. The strings of nuts were dipped into it, hung along a bar in the arbor to drain for a day, then redipped and drained again until six or seven layers were built up.

Whole, a *chuchkella* looked like a lumpy sausage, but when it was sliced into rounds each piece had its own design —an ivory nut encircled by amber rings. In one bite you could taste all of summer.

When it was his turn, Sandro and I took the sheep up to the mountain pastures together, telling each other as we went how brave we would be if wolves should come after the lambs. The wolves waiting at the edges of the forest must have heard us—at least not one ever showed so much as a whisker to us. As he had promised, Sandro showed me the fox den, but the fox and her children were gone. Once we caught a trout but looking at its dappled side, its sad eye, neither of us felt very hungry, so we let it swim away.

We knew when we came home with the flocks, Mamedah would give us an extra good supper, usually a chicken— even if it was Friday.

When Sandro and I teased her and said it was a sin to eat meat on Friday, she always told us, "God keeps his own calendar and He understands if I eat meat today and I fast instead tomorrow."

With the chicken roasted golden brown between two earthen dishes we had a sauce of cornelian cherries and perhaps thin green stalks of wild asparagus that Sandro and I gathered in the hedgerows as we moved the sheep, and always crusty brown bread baked in the deep brick oven in Aunt Salome's garden. And for a little while as we four sat around the table together it was like having a home again.

David could walk and talk now. He remembered me when I came and clapped his hands crying, "Dzma, Dzma." Every time I came I took him walking, and when we were far from everybody all alone by ourselves, I would talk to him about our mother but he could not remember her, or anything of our house. Perhaps it was as well. Aunt Salome loved him as her own and to see him happy with her gave me comfort, but it made me lonely, too.

Aunt Salome asked every time I came if I would not stay with her, but after one day, two at most, I began to think of home and that my father might be back from wherever his work had taken him and perhaps he was missing me and it was time for me to go.

When I was home, all the women in our village were good to me, too, and did what they could—washed my clothes and combed my hair and saw I had a new blouse for Easter.

There were six other boys in the village close to my age, and all of us were good friends. We played games together and went for adventures, but at dusk they would go home— to a mother waiting at the door. If she saw me, she would call me in, too, to eat with them.

"Thank you," I always said politely as my father taught me, but I never went in. I was better in my own house, although I was alone.

Before I ate my supper I fed Challa his measure of barley and brushed his coat and brought him a full bucket of fresh water from our stream and whistled, as horses like you to do, while he drank. Then I divided what I could find to eat with my dogs—one piece of bread for Murka, one for Basar, one for me, one piece of sausage for Murka, one for Basar, one for me.

After our meal was over, the night was long. Sitting by the fire, waiting for my father to come, I remembered how it was before, with all of us there and my mother showing me the letters. I got out our pine board and the marking stick and tried by myself. *A* and *B* and my own letter, *G*, and David's *D*, and *E*, too, I could make, but without a copy I was not sure of the others—was *K* above or below the line? *L*, I forgot altogether. *M* and *N* both had tails, but the tails turned in opposite ways. Did *M* go to the left, or was that *N*? I couldn't ask my father. I couldn't ask anybody.

Then one day Teddua, one of my friends in our village, told me that a man had come to Dushet and opened a school.

"How do you know?" I asked him.

"My cousin will go, and when he learns to write he will be a priest or maybe a tax collector. He is too fat to be anything else. So my father says."

"Will you go, too?" I asked.

"And be shut in a room all day? Not me. I will be a blacksmith like my father and shoe the wildest horses in these mountains."

That would be good work, I had to agree, but I still wanted to learn to read. I asked Teddua where the school was.

"Next to the post office."

My father was away, so next morning early I woke with the sun, brought in wood and fresh water, and put the house in order. I washed myself, smoothed my hair as best I could and tucked in my blouse and started off down the road, my dogs as usual beside me. Halfway down the mountain I began to think—how do I know, maybe a school is like a church and dogs are forbidden.

"You must go back," I said to Basar and Murka. "I am going to a school."

Murka, a sensible girl, obeyed and turned around and started home. Basar laid down and put his nose between his paws and said with his clever eyes, "Let me come, please."

"No dogs go to school."

He flicked one ear.

"At least I don't think they do."

He flicked both ears.

"You are right," I said, "I don't know for sure. But go home until I find out. Home!"

Slowly, as if all his joints ached, he got up and very slow-footed started after Murka.

"Tomorrow," I promised him, "if all goes well and there is no rule against it, maybe I will take you with me."

No one was in the schoolhouse when I looked inside. I walked around Dushet for an hour or more until two boys each carrying a book passed me and I followed after them. Now the school was open. Through the door I saw ten boys sitting on two long benches facing a tall man in a dark coat. On a wall blackboard he began to write letters and numbers with chalk. How I wished I had thought to bring my board and charcoal stick. I drew a little closer to the door and listened.

"And here," the teacher was saying, "is K and L and M and N and . . ."

Of course, now I remembered. The tail of m turned left, and n turned right. I sat down on the lowest step and drew m and then n with my finger in the dust.

The boys were all copying the letters. The teacher walked around the room looking at each slate. As he reached the end of the bench, he saw me, came to the door and looked down at me.

"Who are you?"

I stood up and bowed and said my name.

"Where do you live?"

"Kobiantkari, Prince Teacher."

"Where is your father?"

"He is working."

"At what?"

"Making wheels."

"Does he know you are here?"

"No, Prince Teacher."

"Do you know it costs a ruble a month to come to this school?"

"No, sir, I . . ."

"Do you know that if you come here and listen without paying that is stealing?"

He closed the door.

Stealing!

Inside the boys began in one voice to sound the letters, "*l-m-n-*."

I got up and started back to Kobiantkari.

Stealing? Would our neighbors find out—and lock up their horses when I passed by?

Basar and Murka came running out to meet me, tails wagging. How could I tell them I was a criminal?

"You wouldn't like school," I said. "It's worse than church. No dogs allowed. No people either—unless they give a ruble every month."

For the next few days I asked myself, "Am I really a thief?"

Once Teddua and I stole apples from the orchard of an old man near the military road. Every time I passed his house after that I felt ashamed of myself. Finally, I brought him a sack of nuts from the woods and apologized for what we did. But about the letters I did not feel sorry at all.

I wished I could ask my father if listening was really stealing, but what use? He would only blame himself because he had not one ruble, not even one showre extra, to pay for me at school.

I did tell Teddua what happened. Although he did not understand, he sympathized with me.

"If you like," he said, "I will go with you one night, one dark night, and we will tie a piece of vine tightly across the doorstep and when that teacher . . ."

"No Teddua," I said, "I . . ."

"Or better, we will take plums, very, very soft plums and wait behind the wall until the teacher walks by and . . ."

"That won't give me the letters," I said.

"True. Well I have a better idea. Make friends with one of the boys who goes to the school. Even my fat cousin would do. He will tell you every night what he learned that day."

"No, not that either."

"Then forget the letters," Teddua said, "and be a blacksmith like me."

"Maybe I will."

I gave up any hope of school, and I went to the woods and up the mountainside as before. Sometimes, walking with my dogs, I used to think maybe the teacher was right, maybe I *was* stealing, but just the same I couldn't help being glad I had two more letters, *m* and *n*.

Long afterward, little by little, I finally got the whole alphabet. The next year there was a good harvest, and my father paid a priest two bags of grain to show me the letters in my own name. The rest I learned from Sandro in Muhkran, but *m* and *n* were always my special favorites, and until this day I never forget—*m* bends to the left, *n* to the right.

CHAPTER THIRTEEN

Very soon after my brother David was born, my mother's friend Daro left our village and went with her husband and their child to Vladikavkaz.

I could remember very little about her—except my walk alone to her house and a delicious nine-layered nut cake she used to give me. The neighbors spoke of her often, and from their stories I learned that Daro, like my mother, had brought a great gift to our village.

Although now she was gone from us, we were still proud of her. For Daro was a dancer able to perform the traditional steps with unequaled grace and skill. The Governor General himself had more than once invited Daro and her brothers to appear at the palace in Tbilisi.

Like my mother, Daro also was beautiful. Her eyes, so Dzea Giorgi told me, were jewels, her face as fair as a morning rose.

Two such women in one small place! Of course, they would be jealous of each other and live as enemies; so everybody expected. But everybody was wrong. My mother and Daro became the best of friends. They talked and walked and sewed together.

All this my Uncle Giorgi told me, and he said, "To see them going to the stream carrying their water jugs, to see them in holiday dress their head veils floating—it made the whole village proud. 'Paradise may have the golden streets,' people used to say, 'but it is in Kobiantkari that the angels chose to walk.'"

But not for very long. In the third year of her marriage Daro's husband had a chance to work in Vladikavkaz far away on the northern side of the mountains and she went with him, and not long afterward my mother died. And Kobiantkari had no angels at all.

The years passed, but no word came from Daro. Once, a peddler brought the news that Daro and her husband had gone from Vladikavkaz to Moscow, and there she danced for noble families and earned great sums. But who can believe a peddler? After that we heard from a priest that Daro's husband and child were dead of smallpox and she was very ill. But priests always bring bad news.

That was all until one day when I was about eight or nine years old my father heard from his friend Archil that Daro was coming back.

"Not to the little house across the stream from you where she lived before," Archil said. "No, she has bought a fine vineyard on the mountain slope from the prince, and she will make the old house there into a palace for herself."

The news flew from door to door. The village could talk of nothing else.

"Daro lives!"

"She lives and is coming home!"

"We will have a party for her."

"The biggest party ever—and Daro will dance again for us."

"Just wait," Archil said to me. "Never have you seen such grace. She does not move; rather the earth turns beneath her slippers."

This one told of her goodness, that one of her talent, and all remembered her beauty—her eyes like jewels, her hair dark as a storm cloud over Elbruz, her cheeks fairer than any rose.

"Of course, she *is* five years older now—" said a woman who had newly married into the village.

"What does *that* matter," Miriani, our oldest man, spoke for all. "The rose at noon is sweeter than at dawn. You will see."

No one waited more eagerly than I for that chance, for Daro, I knew, was my mother's own friend, and I hoped she would be mine as well.

Workmen from Vladikavkaz came to make the repairs on her house in the vineyard, finished their task, and went away. The next day we heard that Daro herself had arrived and in her own carriage. The village gave her time to rest before the four chosen to welcome her put on their best clothes, took flowers and fruits and went up the mountain to Daro's house.

Her gate was barred. Her gatekeeper turned them away without a glass of wine, a crumb of bread. That was a scandal. For since we say, "God sends all guests," to refuse the visitor is to deny Him.

Perhaps there was some mistake. The gatekeeper was Russian. He did not understand. People went again, some even a third time, only to be turned away.

The days when Daro danced at the village parties, walked along the village street carrying her water jug were gone. She never came into the village at all—not even once to greet her old neighbors. She had servants to do her errands, Russian servants, who could not even speak to us but only pointed at what they wanted to buy. She invited no one to her house.

The village was bitter. Daro, everyone agreed, had grown proud and selfish and vain. I listened to the talk.

"Spoiled by too much money."

"Yes, and too much flattery."

"And living so long in Russia."

Only my father disagreed. "Perhaps" he said, "she grieves for her husband and child. Wait a little."

A year passed, and Daro still ignored the village.

One Sunday morning my father and I went up the mountainside to her great house. The gatekeeper waved us away.

My father who could speak a few words of Russian said, "Go, please and ask the Lady Princess Daro if she will see the husband and son of her friend—her friend Eamdze."

Not before that, nor ever after so long as he lived did I hear my father speak my mother's name.

The gatekeeper took the message to the house. In a few minutes he came back shaking his head. We, too, were turned away. That *was* the end. Daro was really lost to us, and as time went on, almost forgotten except for a word of gossip now and then.

Once the wife of the druggist in Dushet told someone in our village how many perfumes and creams and lotions Daro sent her servants to buy. Another time the traveling peddler who sold needles and thread and coarse cottons took a special pack from his donkey's back and opening it showed the women in our village what Daro had ordered him to bring from Tbilisi—pins, rings, dress silks that rustled like beech leaves, shoes of soft leather, head veils so fine they floated like clouds in the air.

If the village forgot Daro, I did not.

Soon after her return, I had discovered a way into her vineyard, not through the main gate but across a ravine on a fallen tree and into a woods where her servants came only once a year to cut snelle for grape trellis. I used to dream that one day I would meet Daro walking there and she would know me and sit beside me and tell me about my mother— how she looked and what she said. Maybe Daro would even sing me one of my mother's songs.

A few times I picked bouquets, wild lilies of the valley, sweet daphne, butter-yellow primroses, and just to remind Daro of my mother, dark sweet violets. I always bound the flowers with grass and set them in a holder made of three sticks and left them for Daro on a log near the path. When I went back, I found the flowers in the same place, withered and dry, and so I gave up.

Beyond the woods Daro's vineyards began—black grapes she had, and red, too, and in her orchard were medlars and plums and a whole forest of walnuts. But I never ate as much as one fallen fruit because Daro was my friend or anyway my mother's friend.

All around Daro the land belonged to the prince and on it lived his relative, Cruel Nestor, who managed the estate.

The prince spent his time in Petrograd. For his own vineyard and orchard he cared nothing—except that no one was allowed to touch anything inside his fences. So year after year people went hungry while only a few feet away his grapes dried on the vines and his apples fell from trees and rotted on the ground.

To me this didn't make any sense. Soon I found a way to crawl through a thicket to a break in his fence. Once inside I helped myself to mushrooms and berries and windfall fruits —all I could eat. If I was a thief, well—so, too, were the birds and the foxes who were there before me.

Then one day when I was gathering nuts in the Prince's grounds, I heard horses, and across the fields straight at me slashing his whip came Cruel Nestor himself riding a great black horse and after him a half dozen of the Russians who served him.

When he saw me, he screamed, "Catch the thief!"

I ducked and ran, back into the woods where no horse could follow and under the fence and into the thicket where I thought I would be safe.

But Cruel Nestor and his men circled the woods and surrounded the thicket.

"Get him out!" I heard him call. "Get him out!"

His men began to beat the brush with their crops. I crept to the farthest end and broke through into the open fields. Again they were after me. I ran, I ran like all the frightened rabbits in the world. I knew I could never get home. I turned toward the ravine and ran across the log into Daro's farm.

No horse could make that jump and follow me. I went through Daro's vineyard, keeping low so no one could see me. If I could get by the house, if I could run past the gatekeeper I might get home by the road.

Cruel Nestor had thought of that, too. He and his men circled around, leaped Daro's gate and cornered me by the house. Cruel Nestor's whip slashed across my face. Again and again he struck at me. My eyes were full of blood. I fell, and Cruel Nestor jumped down from his horse and hit me again. His men came up to join his fun.

"Stop," a woman's voice called. "Stop."

I heard footsteps running. Before his whip could fall again a veil covered my head, and I knew I was safe. For no Georgian man, not even Cruel Nestor, would dare to touch a woman's head veil, for us the most sacred of objects.

"He's a thief," Cruel Nestor screamed. "Give him up to me."

"No," the woman said.

"He must be punished."

"No."

One of Cruel Nestor's men jumped off his horse—"I'll get him for you." He grabbed my arm.

"Come away," Cruel Nestor said to the man. "There is nothing we can do to him now. The Lady Princess Daro has saved him, at the price of her privacy."

He jumped to his horse and rode off, his men following. Only after their hoofbeats faded away did I dare wipe the blood from my eyes and raise my head.

Daro did not look at all like Dzea Giorgi said. Her eyes were dull, her hair streaked, her face scarred and pitted from the smallpox that had killed her husband and child.

"This is what I am," Daro said. "Now you know. Soon

everyone will know. Nestor will tell them. Then from memory, too, as from the mirror I will vanish."

I tried to thank her, to say I was sorry I caused her trouble.

"Only for your mother would I have done this—for I knew who you were. I have watched you often from the window. I found your flowers, too."

She looked down and she smiled at me.

Then I understood what Dzea Giorgi meant when he said, "In Paradise they had the golden streets, but it was in Kobiantkari where the angels chose to walk."

For, to me, Daro was the most beautiful woman in the world.

CHAPTER FOURTEEN

After that I went to see Daro nearly every day, and she always called me into the house and gave me white bread and rose-petal jam and cake stuffed with nuts baked in a twist so it looked like a fox curled up to sleep.

She sewed me new blouses; she bought me a pair of real shoemaker shoes. She let me go wherever I wanted on her farm. She took me to stay in her house when my father was away. Best of all, she talked to me about my mother and told me stories of when they were friends—little stories that didn't mean anything, I guess, except to me.

Once Daro and my mother, walking, saw a snake hide itself beneath a stone " . . . and because the whole world hates snakes your mother pitied it, and she brought milk in a gourd and left it for the snake to drink."

"And did the snake drink it?" I asked.

"I think so," Daro said, "but I am not sure. It is a long time since those bright days when we used to walk together in the woods. Your mother loved so much the fragrance of lemon verbena, and once we came on a bush of it in a clearing and we made wreaths for ourselves. She wore hers like a queen."

"Where was I that day?"

"It was before my son, Irakly . . ." Daro's voice always caught on his name, "or you were born."

"Did ever you take us to the woods?"

"Yes, after you could both walk. But I'll tell you another story. One day your mother was stuffing a pillow with goose down when Irakly, playing, ran against her and tumbled the open pillow to the floor and like a whirlwind the house was full of floating feathers. Your mother never said a scolding word to Irakly. She only laughed. . . ."

"Where was I?"

"In your cradle and covered like everything else in the room with down."

"And then what happened?"

"Your mother picked you up. 'See my gosling,' she said, and then she blew the feathers off your face and blanket."

Of course I longed to see Daro dance. But when I asked her, she said, "I wish I could, but after a few steps I have no breath—perhaps one day when I feel better, I will try. You will be my partner."

When Daro saved me from Cruel Nestor, the village knew the whole story by nightfall and they were very proud, of course, and they came again to her door and brought presents.

This time no one was refused, but instead Daro called all her old friends into her house to eat and drink and tell the news and remember the days that were gone. Daro was glad, I think, to be part of the village once more. She took new heart and made great plans. She promised she would pay for me to go to school in the fall.

"Or, perhaps," she said, "I could find a teacher, and we could have a school here in my house and all the children could come."

She was going to build a little house in the village where a nurse could live and take care of very sick people. She wrote to the prince in Russia asking to buy more land from him.

"If he will sell it," she told me, "and I think he will, for he always needs money to gamble, I will rent it to the men in the village for half what the prince charges them now."

But before any of this came to be, Daro grew very pale and tired.

"Go to Skaltupa," everyone told her, "and bathe in the hot springs that bubble from the ground, and in three weeks you will be cured."

She went and there she died. When the news came, the whole village mourned. I missed her most of all, I think, for who, ever again, would bring my mother back crying for the snake, laughing at the flying feathers, running through the woods, standing in the sunlight, a wreath of lemon verbena in her hair.

With Daro, too, died any hope I had for school. My father could not find one extra showre, that I knew.

But maybe I could earn some money for myself—enough at least to buy the rest of the alphabet and even a few words from the teacher.

First, I went into business for myself. I knew a secret place in the farthest corner of the woods where blackberries grew, each as big as a thumb. I lined two big flat baskets with leaves, filled them heaping to the top and put a few flowers around the edge for ornament, and took them to Dushet to sell them.

Nobody, it seemed, wanted blackberries that day. Melons or cherries or quince or apples or green walnuts—that is what I should have brought. I carried my baskets home, still full, and my father and I ate blackberries for supper and for breakfast, too.

"Cheer up," my father said, "you did your best. No man can do more. If you really want a job, I heard of a man in Dushet who wants a boy to help him drive a flock of turkeys to market."

Next day I was hired and off we started. Me—and one hundred turkeys.

Now every animal must have its good points—even a hyena, but it would be hard to pay a compliment to a turkey. Possibly in this world there exists a more stupid, stubborn, contrary bird—if so, Thanks to God, I never had to know one nor herd a flock of them forty miles.

Early, early in the morning we started off down the road with a long wand to keep the turkeys together. But no, turkeys don't want to walk in order. One goes left for a grasshopper; one goes right for a millet seed; a third stops to pick up a sparkle of light; a fourth, threatened by a hawk which is still sitting on top of Mount Kavkaz, squawks and runs for cover and takes all the others along. Forty miles and eight days of this, and we came to the market. The man who hired me was waiting there. He gave me my pay. Twenty

showres! All my own! Even better, he told me that the next
week I was to ride down from Dushet in his wagon and he
would have another job for me to do.

I ran, maybe I flew, all the way home. My father was
feeding Challa. I showed them my wages and proudly I put
the coins in my father's hand.

He would not take it.

"No. It is your money, you earned it," he said, "you spend
it as you will."

I intended to save it all until I had enough to pay for
school, but that seemed selfish. Next day I went to Dushet
and bought my father a packet of tobacco. For David I got
a ball, not a sewed cloth ball, but one of rubber that would
bounce, and a pencil for Sandro, and for Mamedah the best
spool of thread I could buy—not black, not white, but blue,
the color of the gentians that bloom in the fall.

I walked to Muhkran, stopping now and then to take out
my presents and see if they still looked as rich as in the store.
They did. I threw David's ball, but just once because I didn't
want to wear the bounce out.

They all liked their presents. Blue thread, Mamedah said,
was what she had wanted her whole life—and I was the
one who gave it to her.

When I came back to Kobiantkari, I still had two showres
left—hardly enough to save for school. Anyway, I would
earn more the next week. I gave a party for the six boys that
were my special friends. I bought three squares of chocolate
and gave each one half a piece. The gilt wrappers I smoothed
out nicely and kept for myself. For a long time they still
smelled like chocolate.

Monday came, and I was waiting at the roadside when the

cart came over the hill. I jumped up beside the driver before he came to a stop and on we went. The water buffalo were not nearly so smooth and sleek as Pretty One, but they seemed in good heart and flesh and they pulled well together. The driver—his name was Lado—told me he worked every day and sometimes earned two rubles a month.

"Do you think I could work every day?"

"Sure, I know the boss was pleased you got all the turkeys safely to market. The last boy he hired lost thirty along the way. But he would pay you only one ruble—to start."

A whole ruble! Every month! Soon I would be rich. Already I can see myself wearing the shoes Daro gave me and my new blouse and going into the schoolroom. The teacher does not recognize me. I count out my money and pay for one, two, three, four months of school. I sit down on the bench and—

"Are you hungry?" Lado said.

"What? Yes, I guess so."

"Around the next corner is a pear tree with very low branches."

I jumped down and ran ahead. Buffalo carts are good for that. You can get on and off and still catch up with the team.

I filled my cap full of little russet pears and ran back and jumped toward the seat as a hundred times, a thousand times, I had done before but this time I missed the step and fell between the shafts. The great wooden wheel of the cart went over me.

CHAPTER FIFTEEN

The next thing I knew I was home lying on the *tahkte*, and something was tearing my leg from my body.

My father was there, my father's friend Archil, and our neighbors. Mamedah sat beside me, wiping my face. Who told her? Who brought her? I could hear talking, someone crying, voices asking each other what to do. My leg was broken. I knew that. I could see a jagged bone pushed through my skin.

Our village had no doctor. But I heard Archil telling my father that the regiment of Russian soldiers stationed in Dushet had a doctor who came every so often to attend the officers.

"I will go and if he is there I will ask him to come," Archil said.

"But he will want money first," my aunt said,

"Wait—" She took out fifty showres she had been saving a long time, I knew, to buy a new copper jam pot. My father had twenty-five more.

"I will find the rest," said Archil, going out the door, "if I turn bandit on the Military Road. Never fear."

Mamedah covered me and sat down by the *tahkte*.

We waited. I clenched my teeth. I clenched my fists. How long? How long? Mamedah took my hand. Now and then she gave me water from a cup. In two hours Archil came back with the Russian doctor dressed in full uniform, white gloves, bright buttons, and glossy shoes.

"Let me see the leg," he said standing near the door.

Mamedah lifted the cover.

He looked at my leg, at me, at my father.

"The bone cannot now be set."

"But what to do?"

"His leg must be amputated."

"Amputated?" said Archil.

"Cut off."

"Never," my father said, "never. Never!"

"There is no other way."

"Prince Doctor," Archil said, "Greatly Honored Prince Doctor, you are a wise man, a man, it is easy to see, with much experience and education. Surely there is something, something you could try. If it cost extra and we could not pay it today, by next Sunday I would have the rest of money for you. I swear it."

"You asked for my advice. I gave it. Cut off the leg. Nothing else can be done."

"Never," my father whispered.

"I will be frank with you," said the doctor. "Unfortunately, if you do not, he will die."

"Then better let him die," my father's voice came from far away. "What life is there for a man with one leg when I, with two, can hardly support myself? Better be dead than live to crawl from door to door begging your bread."

"As you wish," said the doctor. "Good day."

He went out.

Mamedah began to cry.

"He never even took off his gloves," Archil said, "not even one glove."

The last thing I remember was Archil's angry face as he went to the door and watched the doctor riding away.

"Curse him," he said. "May he live without children and die among strangers far from home."

The pain turned into a wolf tearing at me with iron claws, and then it was a fire burning me up.

"The fever is rising," I heard Mamedah say. "What shall we do?"

No one knew.

At midnight my third grandfather, who had been on a trip, arrived home, heard the news and came at once to see me.

"Over the mountains," he said to my father, "near Chialete lives a man who can help us. I have seen him mend the bones of animals, yes and of birds, too, as good as new."

"Chialete is thirty miles away. You cannot start out until morning. It will take a day to get there, another to come back."

"I will go," said Archil, "and faster than that."

"All day I was on the road," my third grandfather said, "but I will go with you to show you the way. We will go now."

"But the child," my aunt said, "the child cannot—"

"He is not a child," my third grandfather said. "He is a

man." He came and took my hands in his. "You suffer, I know. Try for a few hours more to be brave. Think—in each minute now the Bone Mender is one step closer, two steps, three. . . ."

"Give us cheese and bread and buttermilk," Archil said, and as soon as it was put in the basket they were gone.

Of that long night and the longer day that followed, I remember little—only that at the edge of the blackness I thought I saw my mother and I called and called for her to help me. At last I woke to see an old, old man in a long shepherd's cloak standing beside my *tahkte*.

"Soon, very soon," he said, his voice hardly more than the scratch of one beech leaf against another.

The room was full of our neighbors all asking questions.
"Will you save his leg?"
"Will he live?"
"Can he ever walk?"
"Is it too late?"
"Will his leg be crooked?"

"Go," he said to the women. "Go quickly and get milk, all you can put in the biggest pot you have, and boil it."

As they rushed away, he turned to the men. "Go quickly and bring me twelve bricks and cut me twelve straight branches as thick as my thumb from an ash tree."

The room emptied.

Gently he set my shoulders flat on the *tahkte* and measured my good leg, his hands strong and sure.

"I will tell you the truth," he said, "so you can prepare yourself. In setting your bone I will give you great pain. Forgive me. After that it will be better. When I say 'Now,' take a deep breath and hold it as long as you can. Do you understand?"

"Yes."

"All right. Get ready. Now."

I took the breath—a thousand knives, red-hot knives stabbed me.

"It is over," I heard him whisper. "Your bone is in place—and already growing back together."

The twelve sticks he set around my leg, and wrapped them fast with strips of cloth. The bricks he pounded and mixed with the hot milk to a paste and plastered around and around my leg.

"Now you must not move until it dries. In two weeks I will come again. Meantime," he turned to our neighbors who had gathered around my bed, "go into the deep woods where the lily of the valley grows and dig a basket of the roots and have them ready for me."

The days that followed were long, the nights endless. No matter how I turned there was no escape from the stone prison that held my leg. Our neighbors helped all they could. My father and Archil would raise me carefully so Mamedah might wash me and comb my hair and put a clean shirt on me.

Mamedah made me *ch'hertma*, rich chicken soup frothy with whipped eggs, tart with lemon. When I refused that, she managed to find a good lump of butter and crisp fried potatoes for me. I had no appetite. My leg pained. I was miserable. Everybody pitied me. I pitied myself.

The Bone Mender came again as he promised in two weeks and took off the brick dust cast and half my skin with it, or so I thought. The lilies of the valley were ready for him. He boiled the roots in milk to make a poultice, wrapped my leg in it, and ordered more for his next visit.

While he was there, Sandro came to keep me company, but I did not have any interest in the puzzle he had made for me. I did not want to play knucklebones with him, either. My friend Teddua was there, too, with a whole basket of ripe black cherries.

"If you like them, I will steal more for you," he said. Even knowing they were taken from Cruel Nestor's trees did not give me an appetite.

The Bone Mender ate a cherry, and he asked Sandro to show him the puzzle. Before he left he came close to the *tahkte* and spoke into my ear.

"I will cure your leg. I cannot cure your spirit. That a man must do for himself. Alone. All alone."

I had plenty of days to think this over. When he came again, I told him I would try my best and I did—most of the time.

When Mamedah made me lamb with quinces, I pretended I was eating it with great pleasure, and soon I found I really was.

Dzea Giorgi came down the mountain as soon as we got word to him. He showed me how to make a flute from a thick rose stem and how to play a tune on it, too. He brought a length of cord and taught me to make the knotted frogs and loops we use instead of buttons and button holes on our blouses. I made sets for all my friends. He lent me his knife and he found some pieces of soft wood, and I carved all the animals I could remember and a few I invented.

Every other week the Bone Mender came, walking all the way, to put a fresh poultice on my leg, and I began to worry —so many roots were gathered for me—that the lilies of the valley would never bloom again.

After I was six weeks in bed, the Bone Mender took off the poultice, examined my leg very carefully, moved the knee and ankle and told my father how to make crutches from two forked branches for me.

"Today you will get up. Come slide to the edge of the *tahkte*. Sit up. Pull your legs over."

I did what he said.

"Now stand."

I was half afraid, but he took my hands, and there I was on my feet . . . on my two feet.

The house was full of our neighbors as usual, for as soon as the Bone Mender passed on the road everyone followed to see what would happen, to hear his words, to help if they could.

Now everyone was delighted. They were congratulating me, my father, the Bone Mender and, just for joy, each other.

"He will walk."

"Walk! He will dance!"

"And jump."

"And climb trees."

"And your broken leg will be as good as new."

"Better than new," said Archil. "Much better."

Meantime, the Bone Mender was comparing my legs, measuring by hand spans, from my toes to my ankle, ankle to knee joint, knee joint to hip socket.

"No," he said to Archil. "Not better. Always and always the broken leg will be shorter, shorter by the width of a grass blade . . . for so much he grew before the bone could come together and start to catch up."

The neighbors had brought all kinds of things to eat to make a party in honor of the Bone Mender. Everyone made toasts to him and wished him to live a thousand years and set as many legs. When he was ready to go home, my father left the table for a minute and came back leading Challa.

He put his bridle in the Bone Mender's hand. "Here," he said, "is a small present to take you faster to all who need you as we did."

I wished I was not too old to cry, for I knew my father loved Challa as much as I did.

The Bone Mender patted his soft muzzle. "Thank you. I will take good care of him," he said and I knew he would, for his hands were gentle.

"What a magnificent gift," one said.

"A prince could do no more," said Archil.

"A hundred horses, a thousand horses would be nothing compared to my son's leg," my father said. "It was the best I had to give."

So I could walk again, but, oh, how I missed my golden Challa.

CHAPTER SIXTEEN

By late October I could walk again and I looked for work but found none. The harvest was over; the fruit picked; the turkeys all delivered. Everywhere I went, I had the same answer: "Come back in the spring."

My days were my own. My father was helping a man build a barn at Ananouri, eleven miles up the Military Highway, too far away for him to walk home more than once a week. I kept the house and fed the animals, but as soon as my chores were finished—the floor swept, the wood chopped, the water jugs filled at the stream, the fire banked, a pot of beans set to cook—I was free to go how and where I pleased.

Sometimes my friend Teddua's father, a blacksmith, let us help him at the forge, or my other friend Bootla and I gathered mulberry leaves to feed the thousands and thousands of hungry silkworms his mother raised.

As often as possible, Teddua, Bootla, and I went off to the woods, each of us wearing a willow shoulder basket. If we had patience, we could usually fill at least one of them with filberts or walnuts to divide when we got home.

Into the other baskets went anything else we found, wasp-stung pears, mushrooms, wild grapes, sun-dried to raisins on the vines, blackberries for jam, barberries to season sausage, nettles for soup, gnarled quince to stew with lamb.

Once, as we sat eating our lunch, we heard a loud thumming in the distance. We followed the sound and came to a swarm of bees hanging like a bright melon from a branch. Nearby was a hollow tree trunk full of honey. Although some of it was so old it must have been gathered from the first flowers that bloomed in Noah's garden, we thought it a prize. We lined a basket with leaves from wild grapes and packed in the dripping comb. When we got home, we strained the best part, boiled it down and poured it over nuts we had shelled to make sheets of the golden brittle we call *gozenaki*.

That night there was a full moon, and everybody gathered around a bonfire to tell stories and recite poems, and very surprised and pleased they were when Teddua and Bootla and I came with our trays full of honey candy—enough for all—even a piece to save for each of the littlest children who had fallen asleep.

The next week, full of our success, we went back to the woods thinking to find some more honey and treat our neighbors again.

Although we climbed higher into the mountains than ever before, we had no luck. The bees we tried to follow to their hives led us through brambles, over boulders, into swamps, and then vanished. The day was unseasonably hot for early November, and by mid-afternoon we were tired and dirty when we came to a rocky gorge where the Tergie River makes a green lake before it flows on.

"Let's swim," Teddua said. "Last chance this year."

Bees forgotten, we stripped and plunged in. The rains had not begun, and the water was very low and cloudy. We were too busy splashing and ducking to care. After we tired of that, we dared each other to dive from the rocks above. When my turn came, I hit the water with a loud smack, and I could hear Teddua and Bootla jeer as I went under.

Coming up, I opened my eyes, and there in front of me was a big hole in the cliff just beneath the surface of the water. I put my head out. My friends were laughing too much to notice me. I took a deep breath and went under again and swam in the hole, thinking it probably led up to a cave and I'd hide there a few minutes and give Bootla and Teddua a scare.

What I saw inside shot me out and up through the water faster than any fish.

"Teddua," I shouted and found I had no voice.

My face must have been persuasion enough for he and Bootla caught hold of me.

"What happened?"

"You won't believe it," I said when I could talk again.

"Believe what?"

I pulled them down under the water, motioned toward the hole, and together we swam in and up a little way and came out into a huge stone gallery carved into the heart of the mountain.

From cracks in the ceiling ghostly vines trailed, and a pale green light filled the room. The floor was covered with bones, bleached white, huge bones, ribs that would have made a cage for a hen and all her chicks, hips wider than an ox yoke, skulls like wine jugs with eye sockets our fists could go in, bulging foreheads, huge jaws.

I pointed at the teeth. "As big as a horse's."

"But these aren't horses," Teddua said, "or cows."

"Not water buffalo and not stag," Bootla said.

"I know that. Bones from those animals we saw dozens of times. These are men, I think. Some kind of men."

"Men like us," Bootla said. "Look. They had long arms with five-fingered hands and feet with toes, not paws—"

"And not hoofs." Teddua picked up a leg bone. It was half as tall as he. Carefully, he laid it back. "These men could take apples from the top of the highest tree. Without stretching."

"And cover six feet in a single step," Bootla said.

Looking at the bones, I felt sad. "I wish I had seen them alive, alive and running, wrestling on the grass, sitting around the table eating and drinking and singing."

". . . and dancing," Bootla said. "Dancing they must have made the earth shake."

The light from the roof was fading.

"I think we'd better go," Teddua said.

We took a last quick look around. The eyes in the skulls watched us as we went through the passage and swam to the shore.

Walking home, we could talk of nothing else, of course, but the men in the cave. Who were they? Where did they come from? Why were they buried there? How long ago? We had no answer.

"We will have to ask the Old Men," Teddua said. "If anybody knows, surely it must be one of them."

Now our village had three Old Men who sat on a bench in the sun all day and mended shoes, carved fishhooks, drank wine, answered questions, told stories, and gave good advice whenever they were asked for it and sometimes when they weren't.

Their names were Otar, Vachtang, and Miriani. Otar was a young old man, for he was only ninety; Vachtang was a middle-aged old man of ninety-five, but Miriani was an old, old man who claimed he had lived longer than anything on earth "except maybe a few turtles."

Otar and Vachtang each had a paper from the priest who baptized them to prove their age, but Miriani had nothing at all.

"And for a very good reason," he always said. "I was born before writing was invented."

When we came home, my father was there, and we told our story to him and to the parents of Teddua and Bootla. They, as puzzled as we, agreed that we certainly must talk to the Old Men.

We found them sitting under Miriani's arbor, for the evening was still warm, drinking wine and playing a kind of backgammon we call nardi.

"Be victorious, Princes," Teddua said politely.

After we made apologies for interrupting their game, Bootla said, "If you would be so kind, we need your help."

"With pleasure," Miriani said. "Often when we wanted a pair of young legs to run an errand or carry a message one of you boys was kind enough to lend us yours. Now you need an old head we are happy to lend you ours."

So we told our story again while the Old Men listened carefully.

When we were through, they asked us questions.

"Were their swords and daggers beside them?"

"Any bowls or tools in the cave?"

"Pieces of jewelry or scraps of cloth near the bones?"

"No," we said.

"And the upper leg bone was how long?"

Teddua marked two feet on the floor.

"And the lower one?"

He added another two.

"I think," Miriani said, "you found the Place Where the Giants Came Home to Die."

"Were they men?"

"Yes," Miriani said, "different from us, but men. Long, long ago they lived on earth."

"Some call them Narts," Vachtang said. "Some say they were the first men. We came afterward."

"What happened to them?" Bootla said.

"Slowly, one by one, they disappeared. Nobody knows where or how, for they left no graves, no bones."

"But now I think you found their resting place," Miriani said. "Perhaps as some animals do, the Giants knew when their time had come, and when they grew old or sick they went to their cave to die."

"Did you ever see one of the Giants?" Teddua asked.

"No, but my great-great-grandfather did. At least, he saw a Giant's footprint in the snow up above Mleti."

"Are all the Giants dead?" Bootla said.

Otar shrugged. "So they say, but who knows?"

"I have heard a few, a very few still live at the top of

Mount Kazbeck," Vachtang said. "But unfortunately I never had the pleasure to meet one. At least so far."

News, any news, always spread through our village in minutes. First the women knew and told it to each other in *mahkinjuri*, their secret language that men never learn. Then one woman or another whispered the story to her husband, and he told his brother and he his friend and the friend his nephew and so, I suppose, it happened this time.

Soon Miriani's arbor was crowded with neighbors who asked us more questions and then argued with us and with each other about the answers until the Old Men spoke again.

"Now we know about the Giants," Miriani said, "what shall we do? Keep them a secret?"

To this everybody agreed. Everybody—that is, except Teddua and Bootla and me.

Already we had made our plans to go back the next day and show off the Giants to all our friends.

"The only way to keep them a secret," Vachtang said, "is to forget them." He turned to us, "Will you forget where the place is, what you saw there, never go back again?"

"But why must we do that?" Bootla asked.

"Be quiet; a child should listen and obey," Bootla's father said.

"No, the boys found the Giants," Miriani said. "It is right for them to be heard." Miriani turned to us. "We will listen to you."

"We would never tell outsiders," I said, "nor take them there. But our own friends here in the village, couldn't they go with us?"

"Think," Miriani spoke. "Would you want to see the grave

of your relative, your good friend opened, the bones disturbed?"

"These Giants have no friends, no relatives to care," Teddua said.

"All the more reason then they must depend on us," Otar told him.

"But we didn't know these Giants," Teddua said.

"We do now," Miriani said.

"We would touch nothing," I said. "Only look at them. Now and then."

"True. But going back and forth you and your friends would make a trail that a stranger, if he were curious, might follow to its end, and after him would come others—robbers to see if the Giants had jewels or gold. Priests, Professors, authorities, soldiers, they will all come. Maybe they will even take the bones to Russia and give them to the Czar."

"Why would he want our Giants?"

"Who knows? Thirty years ago, when the Military Road was widened, they uncovered tombs near Pasnaouri, and the officers carried everything they found inside them to Moscow."

"Never will they take our Giants," Teddua said, "not if I can help it."

With this Bootla and I fully agreed, and we all promised to forget the cave.

For quite a while we enjoyed ourselves to be heroes. Almost every door we passed we got a piece of nut cada or a candied plum or slice of corn bread hot from the oven along with a compliment or two and some kind words.

Although Teddua, Bootla, and I were only twelve, the older boys in the village, as a great honor, invited us to join

them for the Berikaoba celebration, the last holiday before
Lent. We chose a leader and made him a goat-skin cloak and
a goat's head with eye slits, a fierce pair of horns and a jaw
that moved when he pulled a string hidden in the chin
whiskers.

At dusk our procession formed with our goat at the head.
After him came the musicians, one playing the bagpipe, the
other a flute. The rest of us danced, hopped, and tumbled
along, singing as we made the rounds of the village. At each
house we "exhibited" our goat, who tossed his horns, waggled
his jaw, kicked his heels and butted his attendants. In payment for our efforts we received a *chuchkella*, some dried
fruits, salt cheese, a few boiled eggs, or, if someone were
very generous or perhaps eager to be rid of us, a few coins.

Our spoils all collected, we made a bonfire and the girls
joined us, and we ate and danced and sang until the flames
died down and the bagpiper ran out of breath, and Berikaoba
was over for another year.

The next day Lent began. From the ceiling we hung a
potato with forty quills stuck into it. Every morning we
pulled one out. That way we could tell how many days until
Easter.

This year it would be a special holiday for us. My father's
younger brother, my Dzea Zacharia, was coming home, his
long service in the Russian army over, and he would marry
a girl from Basalete. The day was set, and on Easter there
would be a party at our house, of course, so the village could
meet the new bride.

Well before the day, Aunt Salome came from Muhkran in
a neighbor's cart piled with baskets full of fruit saved all
through winter, tubs of pickles, rolls of dried cherry paste,

crocks of sour-plum sauce, rose syrup, candied melon rind, strings of marigold flowers, hot sausages, *chuchkella*, and wine from her own grapes.

Immediately we unloaded her stores, Mamedah set us to work. We must scour this, clean that, run here, run there. Rake, hoe, sweep, peel, chop, slice, stir—

"Never will I get married," I said, but not very loud, to Sandro, who came with her.

"Me, neither."

"Be quick," Mamedah said. "Next you must arrange some kind of bench beside the house to set the extra wine jugs on. And after that you must trim back the roses and then a table for the arbor . . ."

We did all that and everything else Mamedah asked, tasting snips and bits as we worked.

On Easter morning my uncle brought my new Aunt Maca home. She was small, hardly taller than I, with dark curling hair, great black eyes, and rosy cheeks. Sandro and I were bursting with pride to have such a beautiful aunt. The whole village, everyone dressed in their best, came to greet them and give Aunt Maca her bride's present, *dzwelli*, we call it, for her new house.

After the company had sung their good wishes to the couple, and they had returned their thanks, we ate and drank and sang again, rested, and began all over.

Sandro and I, if I say so myself, were a big help. For now that I was old enough to give an opinion on village matters and go out with the Berikaoba goat, I must take responsibility for the party in my house and see that all goes well and the guests are happy. So Sandro and I brought more bread and another jug of wine and changed plates and went for more greens and carried wood to roast the *m'tswade* and turned the sticks while it broiled.

I drank a toast to my new aunt and then another one. I never liked wine very much before, but this day it tasted good. Sandro and I each drank some more when we filled the table jugs from the quevre.

Our new aunt danced with me and then with Sandro, and we felt so important we toasted each other a few times. The last thing I remember was Sandro and I in the woods in back of our house, both of us feeling very sick.

When I woke up, it was dark. My face and blouse were wet. Rain? I opened my eyes. No. It was Mamedah pouring water on Sandro and me.

"Over an hour you have been gone from the party," she said. "That is very rude to your guests. Make yourselves clean and tidy and come back to the table in five minutes."

"I feel sick," I said. "Hammers pound in my head."

"In mine, too," Sandro said, "and saws are sawing."

"It will pass," Mamedah said. "You drank too much. The young do this. You have seen puppies take more than their stomachs can hold and then give it back on the ground. Later, as they grow they learn better. When you are men, you, too, will know your own limits. Now get up and wash your faces. In five minutes I need you to help me."

Off she went.

"I can't go," I said. My heart was sicker than my stomach. "How can I face the company? Yesterday they respected me. Now they all know I drank too much."

"Sometime we must face them," Sandro said. "The longer we wait the worse it will be."

We splashed cold water on each other, put on clean

blouses, and slowly made our way back to the table. The party was still going on with toasts and singing. Nobody, it seemed, had missed us. We cleared the plates and brought the cada, the nine-layered cake filled with pounded nuts, and after that jars of candied quince, peaches, and black cherries and the tiny glass saucers to serve them in, and last the copper trays piled high with fruits and more wine.

But Sandro and I did not drink any more toasts; we only raised the glass to our lips.

"For who wants to act like a young dog," Sandro said, "when he is a man?"

A few days after the wedding three strangers came to the village and stopped at the blacksmith shop where Teddua and I were helping his father. The men rode good horses, a blue, as we call dapple greys, a black stallion, a chestnut with a rolling eye, and they had three pack mules in train. But they were not peddlers, not Syrians, not Russians. Although they spoke a language we could not understand, Teddua's father needed no words to see their chestnut had lost a front shoe.

While he brought out his tools, Teddua and I looked at the saddles.

"Never did I see anything like this in my life," he said.

"Leather, flat and slippery as a fish; I think they would slide under the horse's belly. . . ."

". . . or over his tail . . . plunk onto the road."

"Enough," Teddua's father said, in his quiet voice. "If one of you laughs, you will embarrass these strangers and disgrace me, yourself, and your village. Get me more nails."

When the chestnut was shod, one man took out his knife and indicated by gestures they wanted something else.

"Whether he likes to kill us, to eat something or merely

have his blade sharpened we must find out," Teddua's father said.

He gave them a piece of bread but they stood holding it. He tried them again with one or two words he knew in Mingrelian, another Georgian language, then Turkish, and finally Russian. The last seemed to make them talk the most.

"Go," Teddua's father said to me, "and bring your Uncle Zacharia. He learned some Russian in the army. Bring also the Old Men."

They all came back to the forge with me, and my uncle began to talk with the men although neither he nor they spoke Russian fluently.

"They want food," he reported.

"Why didn't they eat the bread I offered," Teddua's father asked.

"Maybe their God forbids them our food," Miriani said.

"Then they would be Persians or Turks or men from our own Dahgestan, which we see they are not," Otar said.

Vachtang had a suggestion. "Let Zacharia ask them if they are infidels?"

Miriani thought that was rude. "If they want us to know they are infidels, they will tell us."

"It is nearly sundown," Otar said. "Suppose Zacharia asks them if they would care to spread their mats and say their evening prayers?"

No, the strangers only wanted to eat—not bread. Other food.

The women, who by this time had gathered around, filled a tray with salt cheese, a bunch of tarragon, eggplant baked with tomatoes, and a roast pheasant and brought it to the strangers.

From his pocket the older one took money and gave it.

This was such a shameful way for guests to act no one knew what to do.

My Dzea Zacharia from embarrassment lost almost all his Russian and only shook his head, no, no, and showed the man he must put the money back in his pocket.

But, no, the man insisted on giving the money.

Finally, Dzea Zacharia found words to explain it was impossible. "All guests come from God! God be praised?"

The man still showed the money.

Miriani had an idea. With Dzea translating back and forth he asked the strangers, "From where do you and your friends come?"

"London."

"Ah, yes, Lahnda. A most beautiful land. Often and often I have heard of it, although at the moment I forget in just which direction it lies."

The traveler pointed toward the sunset.

"Yes, of course," Miriani said, "now I remember. Early one morning very soon my friends and I will saddle our horses and ride there to see its beauty for ourselves—and when we do we will give ourselves the pleasure to visit you and your esteemed family—so meantime please to accept our small hospitality here."

Somehow, when Dzea translated all this, the man seemed more determined than ever to pay us and counted the coins back and forth in his hand.

"This will never do," Kalbatoneh Lucia, the oldest woman in the village, spoke. "These men will stand here and argue until they starve. Zacharia, give them a price—a few showres, anything to satisfy them. It is better that people should say of us we charged guests for food than to say we let them die hungry on our doorstep."

When an Old Man speaks, one listens; when an Old Woman speaks, one obeys.

Dzea Zacharia told the strangers, "Four showres for cheese, ten for pheasant, three for eggplant—and now please enjoy yourself to eat."

No. The men start to bargain. Three for cheese, eight for a pheasant—

"What kind of men are these," we asked each other, "who will bargain for what they will not take for nothing?"

After they finished eating and fed their horses, Dzea talked with them some more.

"In their own country they are scholars, and they make writings which become books," he told us.

"Why do they come here?"

"To climb Mount Kazbek—they have permission from the Grand Duke."

"And from God as well, I hope," Miriani said, "if they wish to reach the top."

"They like also to visit ancient places. They are sure you could show them many."

"Not until we reach the heart of the apple do we find the seed of truth," Miriani said. "Tell them I am a very old man who knows little."

The strangers asked all kinds of questions anyway. Were there old forgotten churches deep in the woods, ruins of watchtowers in the mountains? When we plowed, did we ever turn up a coin, a broken pot, a cup? If any of us had such a thing they would pay well for it—several rubles, and the authorities would never know.

We had nothing.

Georgians were in many wars, they said. Surely an ancestor brought something home—a carved stone, a vase, a buckle taken from the enemy. That, too, would be worth money.

"No one ever brings much home from a war," Miriani said, "except, if he is lucky, himself."

Perhaps we knew of ancient pits where tin or copper was once mined, or old tombs or stone altars, or caves? They would pay five rubles to visit interesting places.

Five rubles! I knew every person there, and I knew exactly what this sum meant to him. To one a better field, to another a doctor for his child, to a third a cow, to my uncle, newly married, a start on a house of his own.

No one spoke. No one so much as glanced at Teddua and me.

A *very* interesting place might be worth more. Perhaps ten rubles.

Ten rubles! I could go to school and maybe find a way to buy back Challa. But what pleasure would I have in an education or a horse if they cost me my village?

"Are you positive there is nothing your people might show us?" the man asked Dzea Zacharia again.

Dzea could answer this question without consulting us.

"I was born and lived here all my life. I give you my word, sir, we have no mines, no altars, no caves to show you—only orchards and fields and vineyards."

On Easter I had wanted to tell Dzea about the Giants, but my father said, "Later. On his wedding day a man has no time for such nonsense."

Now I was glad I waited.

Early the next morning the men rode off and never came back. Our Giants slept on safe in their cave.

$\mathcal{T}$here came a year of drought and after that another and still another. The pastures dried; the earth baked and cracked. Pretty grew thin; her bones were sharp under her loose skin. I gathered handfuls of grass for her along the edges of the dying brook, and when that grew scarce I mixed it with leaves to fool her.

On Sundays in church the priest told us to pray for rain. Although none fell on Monday, the priest made his rounds and took the tithe due him from the little we had. When fall came, the harvest was scant; the wagons rattled home from the fields almost empty. Cruel Nestor sent word he would come for the rents, and if we could not pay them in grain, as usual, then he would take the copper pots.

"Take our copper pots . . ." the word flew around

the village like news of a plague. The copper pot that stood so proudly by each fireplace, polished to a glow by loving hands every Saturday, was a treasure to be passed from mother to daughter and as much a part of the family as the horse, the water buffalo, the dog. More than one woman when she heard the news wasted no time but went to the woods, dug a hole, and buried her pot.

On a hot fall day when a glass sun burned in a glass sky Nestor came for the rents. My father had some grain ready for him, and he made up the rest in cash—although it took all he had saved over the years. Nestor's next stop was at our neighbors.

"Three baskets of corn you owe," Nestor said.

"Not one do I have," Archil said. "Not for you, not for myself."

"You lie," Nestor said.

He poked into every corner, tore the rugs from the *tahkte*, looked beneath it—nothing. Then he saw the copper pot on the table. In it Archil's wife had cooked a stew of pheasant and wild geese, and her children sat waiting to eat their first bit of meat they had seen for weeks.

"I'll take the pot," Cruel Nestor said, and he grabbed the handle and threw the stew out the door.

When Archil's wife saw the meat fall into the dust, the soup trickle away, she screamed and caught up a knife and what she might have done who knows, only her child began to cry and she turned to comfort him. Nestor threw the pot handle over the pommel of the saddle and put his foot in the stirrup. Perhaps the clang of the metal or the woman's scream frightened the horse or maybe he, too, was tired of a cruel master, but just as Nestor mounted, the animal reared.

Nestor, trying to hold on to the pots and the reins lost his balance, fell backwards, hit his head on a stone, and between one breath and the next died. When he was buried three days later, he was punished for all his cruelty and greed. Not one man in the village went to his funeral, and his family had to find strangers, yes, and pay them, what a disgrace, to carry his coffin to the grave.

With Nestor gone we had a few months of peace. We slipped unchallenged into the prince's fields and gleaned a little fallen grain. We picked his grapes. We let our horses and water buffalo and cows in to graze in his fields. If we snared a quail or two or a fat partridge while we watched the cattle, what difference did it make to the prince, eating, no doubt, at the Czar's own table in St. Petersburg. Twice the men killed wild boar in the prince's beech woods, and the whole village feasted on the meat as sweet as nuts.

Things went so well that winter that some people thought our troubles were over—buried with Nestor in his grave. My father did not agree.

"Rent collectors die," he said, "but landlords live forever."

He was right. In March we heard that the prince whom Nestor had served so long was coming himself all the way from St. Petersburg to Kobiantkari.

Although no one, not even the oldest man in the village, knew him, we took heart.

"When our prince sees with his own eyes," we told each other, "that our fields are burnt—"

"—and our water buffalo are thin—"

"—and our fruit trees have died—" "Undoubtedly he will say half the rent—"

"—or a quarter of the rent is enough until the rains come again."

"And perhaps he will build a school—"

"—and pay a teacher—"

So good and kind we made the prince that when his carriage rolled in to the village the day before Easter we welcomed him with wine and flowers and songs from joyous hearts.

He opened his great house and had it made as new inside and out. My father and his friend Archil were called to lay stone for a new walled courtyard with a pool and a fountain.

I went with them—partly to help but even more in the hope of seeing this kind prince who was going to treat us so much better than Nestor. I did see him, for he came out on the balcony almost every afternoon to see how the work went on.

I kept busy, but like a nervous horse I was watching him from the side of my eyes. A handsome man he was, old with his beard and hair frosted white, but he still stood tall and straight and spoke in a voice as strong and deep as a church bell.

One day he caught my glance and beckoned me to come closer. Frightened, I pretended not to see.

"Go," my father said quietly.

I went forward, took off my cap, bowed, and, as was polite, waited for him to speak first.

"What is your name, my child?"

"Giorgi, Your Highness."

"How old are you?"

"Twelve."

"And a great help to your father, I am sure." He smiled and smoothed his white mustache. "Can you catch?"

He tossed something to me and was gone before I could say thank you. I guessed from the wrapping what was inside —halvah. I had seen it in the store in Dushet, and my friend, Bootla, who had eaten a piece at his uncle's wedding, said it was sweeter than honey, richer than butter. Now I would know for myself what it tasted like. I opened the wrapper and broke the halvah into three pieces and laid them nicely on a broad leaf and passed it first to Archil and then to my father. They thanked me but neither of them, it seemed, liked halvah. I ate one piece. Bootla was right. It disappeared without chewing. I put the other two pieces in the wrapper for later.

The prince *was* kinder than Nestor certainly.

After that as we worked the prince often spoke to us, and three times he tossed me candy and smiled when I said thank you.

"Perhaps, living far away, the prince didn't know how Nestor treated us," I said to my father as we were walking home.

"Perhaps," my father said, but he looked doubtful.

That year it was drier than ever. Day after day the sun shone bright as brass. Pastures turned to dust and the stream we called Our Own, a torrent since Miriani, the oldest man in the village had first drunk its water, dwindled to a trickle. September came, but there was no harvest. The fruit we had eaten before it ripened; the few poor nubbins of corn we pulled day by day to keep the animals alive.

The village talked together and chose three men to go on Sunday after church to the prince and tell him we could not pay the rent we owed him. That very night thunder roared in the mountains, lightning flashed, and rain came.

All week it fell like a blessing—slow and steady—filling the wells, waking the pastures, turning our stream into an icy torrent again.

It was too late to save this year's harvest but no matter; we had hope for the future. Now the fields could be plowed again and fall wheat planted. It was a sign. God had answered our prayers. No one doubted the prince would do the same.

On Sunday the three men dressed in their best clothes went to the prince carrying as a present from the village a pot of honey, a few eggs, a small cheese, and some mushrooms. They stood waiting in the courtyard until the prince came on his balcony.

"Prince, hear us!" Irakli, spoke first. "You know the land has been dry."

"And you know, too, we have no crops to pay you for rent—," Challico said.

"Not even enough to keep ourselves through the winter," Kosta added.

"All this is sad," said the prince, "but you do owe the rent."

"If this year you would forgive us, next year we would pay double."

"The rains have come again," Irakli said.

"Impossible." The prince shook his head. "In a week I return to St. Petersburg. I cannot wait. I must have my rents now."

Challico stepped forward. "Six scant baskets of corn is all I have. One I must keep for seed. From what is left, less than a handful a day, my wife, my child, and I must live until spring."

"I, too, must live" the prince said smiling.

"You will live whether we pay or not," Irakli spoke.

"Enough," the prince, his smile gone, raised his hand. "I have listened to your complaints with patience. You owe the rent. You must pay it. There is no more to say."

"Only this," Challico told him. "When you sit at your table, I hope you remember every child in this village cries for food."

"Seize these men!" the prince shouted to his servants. Before anyone could speak again the three were bound with ropes. "Throw them in the stream," the prince said. "Perhaps that will cool their hot tempers." He went back into the house.

The prince's men pushed the three down the bank into the torrent and kept them there all that afternoon. No one dared help them, nor even protest, lest they be thrown after them.

Finally at dusk the prince's men went home, and men from the village who had been waiting pulled the three out more dead than alive. Irakli was so twisted with pain in his legs he could not walk and had to be carried home. Kosta shivered with a chill that never left him until a month later, when he died. Challico, his arms bound, had been washed against the rocks and was bruised and bleeding.

All this I saw. Next day, when my father made ready for work as usual, I did not want to go.

"The prince is worse than Nestor. I wish *he* would fall from *his* horse and die."

"Ssh," said my father, "never say such things. It does no good. We are nothing. To live, bow your head and keep quiet. He pays me. I work. We eat. So it always was—so it always will be."

"Why?"

"Who knows why? Now, come. Today, God be thanked, we will finish the job, and you can sweep the courtyard for me and help carry home the tools."

So we went and I kept busy in the farthest corner, hoping that this day the prince would not appear. But he came on the balcony, and when he saw me he beckoned me to draw closer.

"Would you like some halvah," he asked.

I remembered Irakli, once the fastest runner with the ball at *lelo*, and Kosta and Challico, and I could not speak. I shook my head, "No."

"Ah, you are too shy to say yes today." A shower of silver wrapped packets dropped at my feet. I stood still.

"Pick them up," said the prince smiling. "Don't be afraid. They are all for you."

I shook my head and turned away. The packets glittered on the stones.

"Oh, my poor boy," said the prince very sadly, "I see how it is. Now they have taught you, too, to hate me. Why?"

After that, life was never the same in our village. True, times grew a little better. The prince finally agreed to wait another year for his rent if we would promise to pay him triple the amount due. When he went back to St. Petersburg the new man he left in charge was no worse than Nestor. In fact he was better for us, because he was a gambler who would rather play cards than attend to business. Once we discovered that, he never lacked partners for a game, and his luck was usually bad.

More rains came. The cattle grew sleek again. The harvest was heavy. The carts came creaking home piled with corn. My father was busy every spare minute weaving willow baskets to hold the extra grain. We celebrated and for two days ate and drank our fill.

And yet our world had changed. It was as if the prince had cast not three men but the whole village into the torrent, and we had come out from that cruel baptism with a different spirit to another life.

Many a night I fell asleep on my *tahkte* only to be wakened by my father and his friends sitting close around our fireplace talking, talking. Once a stranger was among them reading aloud from a paper. Drowsily I listened to him explaining, persuading, pleading, and arguing until I slept again.

When I asked what it all meant, my father said, "It was only a dream—for you, for me, for all of us. Many things must be changed, but what can we do? Nothing. Only I am determined you shall not be like me and follow a plow all the days of your life. You must learn a trade."

"Won't it cost as much as school?"

"No, I will find someone who will take you as an apprentice. The work you do for him while he teaches you will pay him for your keep. What would you like most to learn?"

"To make hurt animals well."

"Useless. When a man has no money to bring a doctor for a sick child, who could pay for an animal?"

"To build with stone like Dzea Giorgi."

"That is hard, heavy work for little pay."

My father talked it over with all his friends and they with theirs, and one day our neighbor, Irakli, told us his cousin's cousin knew of a sword maker in Dushet who would take me.

"Sword making!" my father said thoughtfully, "That is

practical and useful and would always give you a living. For surely as long as there are men in this world they will quarrel and need weapons. Would you like to be a sword maker?"

"I guess so."

"In four years, if you work hard, the sword maker says you should know the trade."

It was, everyone agreed, a good offer. Some masters wanted six years of labor and a payment in cash beside.

"This sword maker, thanks to my relative's relative," Irakli said proudly, "will not only take you for nothing, but also he will feed you well. He is, they tell me, a skilled craftsman, and best of all, a good-natured man."

"What do you think?" my father asked me.

I did not particularly want to be a sword maker, but any trade was better than none. Teddua worked all day now with his father at the forge. A few months before Bootla had gone as an apprentice to a leather worker in Dushet. At least, there, I might sometimes see him.

"I'll go," I said.

And so it was arranged. On a cool morning in early September, my few clothes washed and mended and tied in a bundle, my father and I walked to Dushet. The articles were signed with a glass of wine to seal the bargain, and I began my career as a sword maker by sweeping the floor, going for water, cleaning the shoes, washing the dishes, and polishing the copper pots before I went to bed.

CHAPTER EIGHTEEN

*E*arly, early the next morning in that one minute when all the world stands still, waiting to see if the sun will remember to rise again, I heard a jampara bird outside my window. Choodle-eee, choodle-eee. It reminded me of home. I peeked out. Nothing moved in the courtyard.

Choodle-eee, choodle-eee. The jampara called again just beyond the wall. I climbed up and saw Bootla's laughing face.

"No jamparas in this place, choodle-eee, but me. Well, what's he like?" He nodded toward the house.

"Very hungry and very thirsty and very fat and, I think, very lazy. Yours?"

"Stingy. He counted every bean I ate last night. He expects us to work from dawn to dark. He'll be looking for me now. I must go. It's four streets away. The first chance I get I'll come again. Listen for me."

He drew the shadows around him like a cloak and disappeared. At the end of the street a jampara called and then farther away another answered.

I went back in the house and emptied the ashes, started the fires, swept more floors, brought more water, and polished more pots. As the days went by, I progressed so far I was cooking the meals, keeping the garden, and waiting on the table when the sword maker had parties for his friends.

The first weeks I felt as lost as a blind man dropped in a well, for there were no sounds, no scents to give me a clue to life, no cock crow to say day had come, no whiff of smoke from the neighbor's chimney to tell which way the wind stood, no creaking cart to let me know my father was coming home. But slowly I grew used to the stagnant air, the clamor in the streets, the strange faces, and I told myself (sometimes I almost believed it) that this was not too bad a life. Other apprentices on our street had masters who cursed and starved and overworked and often beat them. My sword maker was good-natured even when he was drunk, which was most of the time.

His wife, poor woman, did what she could for me, but she had three small children and a baby to attend. I had a room to myself, a closet really with a slit of a window, behind the kitchen. My bed was a stone shelf, but I made it softer with pine branches under my blanket. There was enough food— more than enough. That was the trouble.

Better than anything else in life the sword maker liked to eat and drink, and friends he found in plenty to keep him company around his table every night. All apprentices were expected to carry in charcoal for the fires and fill the water jugs and pails from a tap at the end of the street. I did that, of course, but I also had to run to the market for nuts, for onions, for chickens and soon I was peeling the onions, pounding the nuts, cleaning the chickens and before I knew it mixing the sauce and roasting the chicken as well. At the end of six months about all I had learned of sword making was how to sharpen a boning knife.

The pity of it was that the sword maker was a master of his craft. When he felt like working, no man in the town, no, not in the district was his equal. He tempered steel with a sense of timing beyond sight or scent or sound; he could fine a blade sharp enough to cut a floating feather, and at chasing a design on a hilt he was a true artist.

I would have kept the hearth glowing all day and never counted myself tired if only I could have worked with him in the shop. But seldom did I have a chance. In the morning he slept late, tired from the night before. I always cleaned the shop nicely and set the brazier glowing and laid out the jobs on hand, hoping he might look in when he woke and take a notion to work. If he did, I could enjoy myself for an hour or two helping him. To watch the metal take form beneath the hammer and then bloom in the fire from grey to cherry red seemed a miracle to me—one worth any effort to achieve.

But sooner or later the sword maker's friends drifted in, and then it was always the same. "Watch the forge," he would say, "for a few minutes while I go across to the *duquani* for one glass of wine."

Soon the charcoal was finished. The fire died. The steel cooled and not until night would the sword maker come back arm and arm with his friends, all of them ready to eat and drink and sing the night away.

When I first began my apprenticeship, people still ordered new daggers and swords, but as all they got were promises, which they could not wear on their belt, they stopped coming. A few men still brought in a knife to be reset in a handle or a blade to be honed, but soon they, too, grew tired of waiting for what was never done and finally took their work away.

Sometimes, if the sword maker and his friends got drunk early enough and fell asleep, I slipped out and went to see Bootla for a few minutes.

About once in three months we had a day off to go home and see our family and friends. Bootla's parents and my father came now and then to Dushet to see us, but frequent visits were not encouraged on the theory it made apprentices homesick, discontented, and restless.

On Sunday, when we had a few hours in the afternoon for ourselves, we took bread, and I could usually get a piece of meat as well, and we followed the road a little way toward home to fool ourselves. When we came to a good place we knew beside a creek, we made a little fire and roasted our meat and talked.

Bootla's master, the leather worker, wasted no time or money on drink and very little on food. His shop, which specialized in crops and bridles, was the biggest in the town with a journeyman and three other apprentices older than Bootla. The hours were long and the work hard. Except when he went for water or delivered finished pieces Bootla hardly left his bench. Already he knew how to use the drawing knife, the awl, and make ornamental braids.

Sitting there on the hillside, munching the hard, sweet

wild apples we gathered, we talked of what we would do when our apprenticeship was over and we were masters of our trade.

"We'll stay two years," Bootla said, "or even three."

". . . and earn good wages and save every penny until we have enough to go home in style."

"With new *cherkasskas*, tailored from the best wool cloth. And I will make us each fine daggers. . . ." I said.

". . . and I the belts to hang them from. And new boots . . ."

"Of course, we must buy presents for everyone in the village."

How glad they would be to see us home; how surprised to find us men, men with a trade, men dressed in fine clothes.

"Perhaps no one will recognize us, and we will be greeted as strangers. How we will be laughing when Teddua calls us 'prince'!"

So we planned when we were in good spirits, but if it had been a bad week with Bootla's master hard to please and my sword maker drunker than usual, then we considered a different future.

"Maybe we should run away," Bootla said, "to the mountains and be brigands. Then we wouldn't have to spend our life in a dark room in a dirty town."

"My father would be ashamed if I took what was not mine."

"We'll be the kind of brigands," Bootla said, "that steal only from the rich. In fact we'll make it our habit to steal only from rich Russians. Nobody would mind *that*."

"My aunt would. She is against stealing from *anybody*. If she knew I was a thief, she would find me if I was hiding in the highest tower on the highest mountain in the world and make me give back everything I took."

"That would make problems. How about being hunters

instead? We could track down snow leopards and mountain tigers, and foreign gentlemen would buy the skins for a hundred rubles and say *they* shot them."

"I don't like to kill animals, least of all what I don't intend to eat. I wish there was some way we could be heroes of some kind, but I suppose that takes longer to learn than sword making."

So we stayed on, apprentices at our trade. The first year passed.

On New Year's Day, 1914, my sword maker had a party for all his friends, and, sitting at the table with his glass in his hand, he fell dead. I felt sorry, of course, for his wife and his children, and I pitied myself, too. My year and a half with him was all wasted, or so I thought then. And now what was I to do? Go back home with half a trade? Never! Stay on? How? The sword maker's wife decided at once to close the shop and go to live in her father's house. There was no other sword maker in Dushet.

While I sat in the empty shop beside the cold forge I heard the jampara call beyond the gate. I opened the door to Bootla.

"Come quickly," he said. "My leather worker says he will talk to you and if all goes well maybe take you into our shop. Two of our apprentices have finished their time. And I . . ." he drew himself up proudly, ". . . personally guaranteed you."

"But of leather work I know nothing—except how to make a bridle for my own horse."

"You will learn. I'll help you."

I put on my Sunday blouse and tucked it in neatly and combed my hair and off we went.

The leather maker wasted no words. "Bootla says you want to learn our trade."

"Yes, sir."

"Are you lazy?"

"Sometimes, I suppose I am."

"I am sure of it. All boys are lazy. But you, at least, are honest. I will talk to your father, and, if he agrees, I will try you for a month. . . ."

"Thank you. I'll . . ."

"And if you are not too lazy or too slow, I will teach you the trade in three years. While you learn, I give you nothing but your food and a place to sleep."

"Thank you. I appreciate . . ."

"Work not words speak to me." He went back to the bench.

I had a bed in a room with Bootla and another apprentice, a Russian boy named Sergei, who was not happy to see me.

"Already too crowded here with too little to eat, and now you have come it will be worse."

"I'm sorry," I said. "I will try not to take anything that is yours."

"Don't apologize to him," Bootla said to me in Georgian, "He is jealous. He wants to be the only leather worker in the world."

"And you will be talking together in that language of yours," Sergei turned up his lip, ". . . ghh, khh, kkkgg . . . like monkeys chattering."

"Forgive us," said Bootla as politely as he could in his broken Russian, "if we have made you lonely for your friends."

Sergei's answer was to go out the door and slam it behind him.

My new master, I discovered in the next few days, was very unlike my old one. He never wasted a minute's time in a *duquani* or sitting around the table. He fed us as cheaply as he could, although I will say for him he ate what he gave us. He was not an easy man to please. The knife must be held just so; the strips cut exactly straight; the awl set plumb for each punch. Back he sent even rough thongs to be trimmed over—two times, five times, but when at last he said, "Good enough," it was worth the trouble.

Altogether I liked it better than the sword maker's. The shop was a busy one. The journeyman named Leo, who had finished his time two years before and now worked for wages, was good-natured and patient and ready to show me what he knew, and as the weeks passed we grew to be good friends.

Sergei still resented me. He complained I crowded him at the bench, I dulled the knives, I stood in his light, I smudged the leather, until finally the master said to him, "Be quiet, Sergei, I have eyes."

That made Sergei madder than ever. One day, when the master was gone, he began to quarrel with Bootla over some foolish thing.

"If you don't like us," I said to Sergei, "I propose we have a fair fight. Either Bootla or I will wrestle you any Sunday you please. You can name the time and place and bring your friends."

"And win or lose I will buy you all a glass of wine afterward," Bootla said.

But to this Sergei would not agree.

"Coward," Bootla said.

"Less talk and more work," Leo was stern, "or the master will blame me when he comes back, and then you will all have broken heads . . . and no wine to follow, I promise."

That night it was my turn to bring water from the tap.
Coming home I saw Leo waiting in a small passage between
two houses. He put his finger to his lips and beckoned me to
follow him. When we were hidden by a bend in the wall, he
stopped.

"Listen to me. You and Bootla be careful, very careful with
Sergei. He can do you much harm."

"Who's afraid of *him.* . . ?"

"*You* should be. Don't anger him. His aunt is the maid in
the house of the Russian commander of the garrison, and she
has the ear of the commander's wife. If there is trouble, they
will believe Sergei or rather his aunt. Not you. Remember
what I say and tell Bootla."

I did.

Bootla laughed. "If he would run and ask his aunt for
protection, he's not a man, not even worth a fight."

After that we paid very little attention to what Sergei said
and did and that for some reason only made him worse.

As the weeks turned into months, the leather maker gave
me finer and finer work to do—braided crop handles became
my specialty. Leo said that I would soon catch up to Bootla.
In any case he planned to stay on as a journeyman until my
time was up, and then what? Should we go to Tbilisi as we
dreamed? Or stay on here until we saved enough money for
a shop of our own someday—with our name in golden letters
over the door?

July came. Bootla had only one month more as an ap-
prentice. Suddenly the work in the shop began to pile up.
Bridles, saddle girths, crops; all at once every officer in the
Vladikavkaz garrison needed new equipment or old gear re-

paired and gave Bootla and me ten, even twenty kopecks to deliver their orders to the barracks the minute the job was finished.

In no time we had made a ruble between us, and we took turns carrying it in a leather purse. Every time Bootla counted it, which was at least twice a day, he always said, "I can see the gold letters over our shop shining in the sun."

"Why is everybody in such a hurry?" I asked Leo one day.

"Some kind of an archduke was killed."

"Where?"

"Who knows. Far away someplace."

"Why was he killed?"

"Who knows?"

"There must have been a reason."

"You don't need a reason to kill an archduke."

"But what has that to do with all the extra work brought in the shop to be finished at once?"

"The officers hope to make a war out of the dead archduke."

"Why a war?"

"Why? To earn promotions, naturally, and medals and estates and prizes."

"It doesn't make any sense."

"Of course not," Leo said, "and in any case it is no business of ours. See—while you are busy asking questions you have cut your strap too short. Start another piece."

We had to put in extra hours at the bench. Tempers grew short. Bootla reaching for an awl accidentally touched Sergei's arm. Sergei cursed him. Bootla gave him another shove, this time on purpose. Sergei in a fury threw his knife at Bootla, who ducked, and the blade went hilt deep into my wrist.

My first thought was surprise that Sergei could hit anything, my second, relief that the master, away on business,
couldn't see my blood running down on his leather, and my
third, a hope we might be able to clean it up before he came
back.

"Quick, Bootla, get me a piece of rag."

But Bootla in a fury was chasing Sergei around the room,
and before Leo could calm them Sergei tripped over a
saddle, struck his head on the bench, and fell flat on the
floor.

"Let him alone, Bootla," I said. "It was an accident. Bring
me water in a bucket. . . ."

"Get up, coward," Bootla said. "My friend excuses you.
You are safe."

Sergei didn't move.

"Get up," I said. "Let's forget it all."

No sign that he heard.

Leo tried to raise him, but he was as limp as a rabbit.
Bootla, back with a bucket of water, poured some over his
face.

The leather worker came in, took one look, and without
a word brought brandy from a cupboard, and poured some
into Sergei's mouth. Most of it ran down his chin.

"Is he dead?" I said.

"I don't know." The leather worker put his ear against
Sergei's chest and listened. "He breathes. Chances are he's
not dead. Yet. What happened?"

Leo told him. "It was Sergei's own fault. I saw it all."

"That makes no difference. Whether Sergei lives or dies,
Bootla will be in prison before the sun sets if he stays here.
Sergei's aunt will see to that. Quickly, Bootla, leave here and

disappear. Go home, go anywhere; keep out of sight until we see what happens."

"Never will I run," Bootla said. "I did what any man would do who saw his friend stabbed. I will tell Sergei's aunt and the commander and the judge and the Czar himself the truth. . . . "

"You will have a chance to tell nobody," the master said, "except the guards who take you to Siberia. Listen to me! For a day or so Sergei will not remember much, and by then you will be far away. In a few weeks his apprenticeship is over, and I will find him a good place with a friend in Vladikavkaz if he will forget the whole thing."

"No."

"If you stay you will make trouble for yourself . . . for me, too, and before this is through bring us all to prison."

Bootla rolled up his tools in a piece of leather and tied them with a thong. "Then I will go."

"If you go, I go too," I said. "Gather my tools for me."

The master put a great loaf of bread, a round of cheese, and a piece of ham in a goatskin bag and stuffed the few belongings we had on top of it. He brought some coins from his pocket.

"Here's a ruble for you."

Leo found a strip of cloth and bound up my wrist. "Someway we'll get word to you in your village. Until then keep out of sight. Now, go. Quickly."

It was almost dusk and the streets were empty. Inside the houses we passed candles flickered and fires glowed. Whiffs of roasting meat, frying onions drifted out.

"I'm hungry," I said.

"I am, too."

Yet we knew we dared not stop for so much as a bite of bread. Already we felt pursued and kept close to the shadows of the walls until we came to the outskirts.

"Now which way?"

"We can't go home. The village is the first place they will look for us."

"Let's turn west and follow the ridge. That will lead us around the village and up into the mountains where we used to go."

"No path along the ridge, and sharp drops on either side—"

"So much the better."

On and on we walked while the stars came out and the moon rose. Not until long after midnight did we come to a place we knew between two cliffs. There at last we dared to rest and eat our bread and some cheese.

"Remember how we were going home?" Bootla said. "With presents? With fine clothes? Here we are—I'm a hunted criminal. And I made you one."

"Nothing to do but make the best of it," I said. "Let's eat the ham, too."

For the next three days we moved up and down the mountainside, piecing out what we had with anything we could find. We made a dam and diverted a shallow stream and caught three trout and grilled them on sticks over a quick fire. We discovered some cress and a few sour plums. Neither very filling.

My hand was giving me pain. I slept little. By the fourth day my whole arm had swollen. Our bread was gone. We had nothing for our supper but two not very fresh pheasant eggs.

When night came, we crawled into a rhododendron thicket. I ached all over, and every move was another knife thrust in my arm. When at last I slept, I dreamed I was eating sausage, hot, the skin bursting. As I took big bites, I could smell the smoke from the cooking fire, hear the fat sizzle as it hit the coals. I opened my eyes. The dream kept on.

Bootla roused, sat up. A branch snapped. We both froze like rabbits.

"If I were a policeman, you'd be halfway to the jail by now," a voice said. Teddua's!

We rolled out of the thicket. There he sat on a flat rock broiling meat with a basket full of bread, cheese, and fruit beside him.

"How did you find us?"

"Leo sent word to the village—about what happened. I knew if you were hiding it could only be here. Yesterday I came and in one hour I found your tracks. Like two bears passed by!"

"Are you sure you were not followed?" Bootla asked.

"Very sure. No one wants you. You can come back whenever you like."

"Sergei, isn't he dead?"

"No—but gone to Russia—with his aunt and the commander's wife and the commander—the whole garrison. There is a war. Men are called up. Soldiers are marching day and night over the military highway."

"Who attacks us? Turks? Persians?"

"Neither. It is not our war. The Czar quarrels with some of his own friends, I guess. Leo said to tell you to come back to work at once."

Bootla did. I got only as far as the village before I toppled over. Teddua's mother put me to bed and made a poultice of an herb, comfrey, I think it was, something slimy and green, and she plastered my arm with this every few hours until the pain stopped. Slowly I recovered. Although the wound in my wrist healed, I had little strength in my fingers, and until I could use the tools again it was no use to go back to the leather worker's. I stayed on in the village, helping one neighbor and another with the harvest, for many men had been taken into the army. The age was lowered. Soon my turn, too, would come.

In late October I was called up. I was to leave on Thursday and report to a garrison fifty miles north on the military highway.

I walked to Muhkran to say good-bye to Mamedah and David. Sandro had already gone. I went to Dushet to my old shop. Bootla had just received his notice to report at the local army post. Leo shook my hand warmly. Even the leather worker had a kind word for me.

"The weeks you still owe me on your apprenticeship, I give you for a present. You are now a journeyman. Here are your papers. Keep them. If you have the good sense to stay alive, you will find work waiting for you here when the war is over."

Last I went to see Miriani.

"What can I tell you?" he said. "It is a hundred years now since I fought against the Turks." He thought a while. "But I suppose a soldier's life is about the same. You will walk more than you shoot, so take as much care of your boots as your gun."

I said that I would.

Miriani sat quietly for a few minutes before he spoke again. "For centuries and centuries you know we battled

Turks, Persians, those we call infidels. They were our ancient enemies, yet when they had finally driven all the Crusaders out of the Holy Land they made us the Great Gift Forever— a promise that so long as Moslems controlled Jerusalem out of all Christendom only we Georgians might enter the city wearing our side arms with all our banners flying. Do you understand why?"

"I think so," I said. "Because they respected us?"

"Yes. When you are a soldier, do not forget you are first a man. So, too, is your enemy."

"I will do my best."

He kissed me. "Safely go and safely come. We will be waiting for you."

The next morning I set off. The whole village had gathered. The women gave me small presents—a boiled egg, a few pins, a round of corn bread, *chuchkella,* two needles full of thread to mend my clothes, a wooden comb, a packet of dried persimmons. My pockets were full. The men and the boys joined my father and me and walked along "for company" as we took the path that led to the military highway. At the top of the hill I turned and looked back. The women still stood at the gates watching me, as I had watched others go from home. I waved good-bye to them all, good-bye to my golden Challa and to my dogs that were gone, to Pretty One chomping her last oats from my hand, good-bye to part of myself I was leaving in the village.

By mid-morning we were well north on the military highway that runs from Vladikavkaz to Tbilisi. At noon we came to a small *duquani,* or wine shop, called the Inn of Sorrows, for here friends and families made their last parting with those leaving home for Russia.

We sat under the arbor and ordered some wine and ate the bread and cheese we brought from home. When the owner heard I was going to war, he gave us free a plate of fresh greens, tarragon, cress, and new onions. Our neighbors drank to me, touching my glass in turn, wishing me to be well and to come safely home.

All too soon a cart creaked into the courtyard. The driver agreed to take me over the pass. My neighbors kissed me. Last my father took me in his arms.

"Keep a good heart," he said.

I climbed up beside the driver, and we were on our way.

"Be victorious," I heard the voices calling after me. "Be ever victorious!"

From the mountainside the echo joined the chorus, "Ever victorious, victorious."

CHAPTER NINETEEN

*N*ow, more than forty years later, I am walking the road once more to my village. The scent of the lemon verbena from the hedgerow, the loam beneath my foot, the checkered flash of the magpie, the pipits' fluting call all tell me I am really here.

At the bottom of the hill Levan was waiting in the car to pick me up.

"I took the others on," he said, "and left them at the house, but I was afraid you could not find your way. . . ."

"Me, not find my way?" I thought. "Me, who knew it through rain and snow and the darkest night?"

But to be polite I got in and said nothing. As we drove along I saw Levan was right. I felt as if I had stepped through a mirror. In Dushet the old post station had disappeared, and in its place was a new school. The bakery was now a clinic, the old market transformed into a park. Something must be left untouched. The sword maker's?

"I'm sure I can find the place I learned my first trade," I said to Levan. "Turn right. Then left. There beyond the corner?"

Levan slowed down.

"The next time I want to have my mustache curled, I will surely call you," he pointed to the sign.

"Beauty shop! Well—a better business than making swords anyway. Maybe I can find the leather worker's."

We drove up one street and down the next, past apartments, stores, cinemas—the old stone shop had vanished.

"I give up," I said to Levan. "Let's go to the village."

When we arrived at the stone house above the stream, where Irvandis' wife, Nina, and their son Nougzari lived, we found a crowd of relatives, friends, neighbors in the yard. Across the hillside I could see more coming. Along every path people walked, moving toward the road that led to the stream crossing and this spot.

I got out of the car and was caught in a whirlwind. As at the airport, I scarcely had time to recognize a face, catch a name before I was caught again and again, and new arms embraced me, new voices joined the chorus of "home at last, home at last."

Slowly I made my way to the house, up the steps, across the long veranda, where Helena stood talking with a tiny woman in widow's black. My Aunt Maca. If the rosy cheeks and black curls were gone, her eyes had lost none of their dark brilliance since I danced with her on her wedding day.

I knew that Dzea Zacharia died long before my father and that she had lost two sons in the Second World War, but beside her now stood a tall man who enveloped me in a bear hug—Aunt Maca's grandson, who has both my names.

Friends pressed around us. Slowly I began to sort them out. Some I recognized because a child's brow, a boy's smile still lingered in an old man's face. Bootla's mother I knew the moment I heard her laugh, Archil's wife by the faint scar on her cheek. Often it needed only a word or two to roll away the years.

"Want to go up the mountains?" someone in back of me asked.

I would know that voice anywhere. I wheeled around. Teddua. It made me laugh to see him standing there, for surely he must have clapped on this white hair and beard to play a joke on me.

After him came Bootla's father, handsome and dignified as always, and not one bit changed since I saw him last. I started to greet him respectfully, using the formal person, when he burst out laughing and I realized my mistake. It was not Bootla's father, but Bootla himself.

"Just how we used to dream it would happen," he said, "only we never thought it would be *you* who didn't recognize *me*."

We had little time to talk. More and more old friends kept arriving, and soon we heard Irvandis' wife calling us inside.

"Come. Come. Be so kind as to all sit down."

"Come. Come," said Zina and Eterre in a kind of chorus. "And we will eat a small bite."

It took some maneuvering to follow their orders, for, as Helena said, they must have built the room around the table, leaving a narrow margin for sitting space.

A banquet was spread before us. Dishes and bowls and platters and trays, each one piled high, each one adorned and garnished.

"As your sisters kept assuring me," Helena said, "when I proposed we bring a sandwich—'no need to worry, something will be arranged'—although it must have taken a crew of twenty working around the clock all week to accomplish this."

Exactly what we ate I cannot remember. Later I asked Helena.

"The answer is simple," she said. "Everything. I don't think there is an edible material that walks, runs, flies, swims, grows above or below ground that was not offered in some form. All of it prepared with the greatest love and skill and presented as if it were an entry for an art exhibition."

Once we were at the table I had a chance to talk with my old friends. We exchanged our histories since we parted; we threw "do you remembers" at each other until our eyes were full of tears from laughing and weeping. We told old stories. We remembered absent friends.

Many faces I missed. A few, a very few, had moved away. Others were dead—old age, illness, accident, and, of course, the war. Often when I mentioned a name the answer was, "at Stalingrad," "missing after Sevastopol," "outside Moscow."

"What happened to the Old Men?" I asked.

"The two youngest died first," Teddua said, "and Miriani last."

"But before that happened," Bootla added, "many doctors came to interview him. Every word he said they wrote down, and they took his photograph, too."

"Did he ever tell them how old he really was?"

"Not them. But the year before he died he told Teddua

and me, 'If I live until Easter, and I always do, I will be one hundred and twenty-six my next birthday.'"

"But after his funeral," Teddua said, "as we were eating *sheelah pilavi* in his great-great-granddaughter's house, Kalbatona Lucia, remember her, told us when she was a child her oldest brother and Miriani were best friends. Both had their twenty-first birthday the year the great star fell."

"The meteor—" I counted. "That would make him only one hundred and twenty-three."

"I think it was an honest mistake," Teddua said. "He would not lie."

"I agree."

"I, too," Bootla said. "Let us drink to him. After all, three coins are nothing to a man who has all his pockets filled with gold. So it was with our Miriani. What did three years, more or less, mean to him, rich as he was in days and months, in sunrises and sunsets, in blossoming springs and golden falls? He did not need to count them over like a miser, he who had so many."

We dipped a crust into our glass as we do when we drink for the dead.

"To Miriani."

"Who are the Old Men now?" I asked when we put down our glasses.

"Irakli and Challico."

"And that reminds me," Teddua said, "it is time for us to choose our Tamada who will lead our toast. Who better than the oldest and wisest among us. Irakli."

A good choice, the whole table agreed, and he was selected.

Meantime, full dishes replaced empty ones. Glasses were

filled and refilled. Irakli accepted his office with an appropriate speech. With the proper precedence he began his toasts, drinking in turn for each one present. He knew exactly what to say. As a jeweler takes up a stone and turns it this way and that to let the facets catch the light, so Irakli chose the best qualities in every man and held them up to view.

I moved around the table and sat beside him for a little while, and we talked about the old days.

"What happened to the prince's farm?" I asked him.

"After the Revolution it became a collective—fruit and grapes. I was the manager until I retired."

"And the prince?"

"Who knows? He never came back."

"He almost killed you."

"True. Nevertheless, here I am. He thought the weapons and the power were all his. He is gone. The village survived."

"This is as good a time as any to satisfy my curiosity," Helena said. "What became of the man who rose from the dead?"

"Dadico?" Irakly said. "Nothing. He lived another forty years and had the most beautiful orchard you could hope to see. When he was about eighty, he died the second time and that time, unfortunately, he died permanently. We had his second funeral—not such a happy one, naturally, as his first."

Time for more toasts, more music, more talk. We drank to those who were absent, to Helena's relatives, to the new friends I had made, to my new country, to our own fertile land, to peace in the world.

Never, I guess, was there a bigger or better party in our

village. Before the day was over, more than a hundred people sat at the table—not all at once, true—but after an hour or so a few would leave to walk in the garden, a few others would join us.

As the women came in, each one set a gift down before Helena—a jar of candied apricots in syrup, a roll of dried peach leather, a setting of four duck eggs, two perfect pears.

"How can anybody keep pears unblemished for six months without cold storage?" she asked me.

"Tie a string to the stem and hang the fruit from the ceiling in a cool room—or bed it in soft hay and turn it every day."

After the pears came equally beautiful apples, a jar of shelled walnuts and a bag of whole walnuts to plant, pickled eggplants, pomegranates, a piece of bacon cured to pearly translucence, a string of dried marigolds for flavoring. The pile kept mounting.

"I'm overcome," Helena said. "It's too much. Just because I'm a visitor . . ."

"No, no," I told her. "You don't understand. It's because you're *not* a visitor. All these presents are your *dzweli,* your 'bride's gift.' Every girl who marries in the village receives her *dzweli* to start housekeeping."

"Then I must thank them," Helena said, and so she did. That her Georgian was limited seemed to trouble no one.

"Could you understand?" I asked Bootla when she finished.

"Certainly. Very simple. I listened to what Kalbatono Helena meant, not what she said."

The happy hours passed. We talked of old times and old friends. We laughed; we wiped away the tears; we laughed again. We sang; we danced.

Irakli had finished all the official toasts. Now, with his permission, anyone could propose his own.

I raised my glass.

"I drink to our village. Like all of us who are here, I loved it, but I never knew how much until I went away. Through the war and the time afterward, half-starving in Persia, in Turkey, and the first years in America, going from job to job, often I was sad, often I was lonely, but never, as I saw others around me, alone. For wherever I went I knew that here in the village I still had my place. Here you still spoke my name. Here I was remembered."

It was long after midnight when the party ended. The car was waiting to take Helena and me to Tbilisi. The rest of the family would follow in the morning.

Teddua, Bootla, and my namesake, Maca's grandson, rode along with us "for company" to the top of the hill. There we stopped for last farewells.

"You must stay," Bootla said. "Before too long you and I and Teddua could be the Old Men."

Teddua laughed. "Of course, you must stay. But we are far too young to be Old Men. I have a better idea. We'll put on our shoulder baskets and roam the mountains as before. Who knows what we may find?"

"I would like that," I said, "but I cannot stay. My home, my work, my life is in the United States now."

Bootla took my hand. "Of course. We understand. We rejoice in the success, the happiness you found there. But do not forget us, and come back soon."

"Very soon, if possible," Teddua said, "but whether soon or late, the village will always be here."

About the Author

George Papashvily was born in Kobiantkari, Georgia, in 1898, and emigrated to the United States in 1922. He traveled all over the United States, working variously as a farmer, in a factory, as a mechanic, and in many other trades, while he laboriously learned English. In 1933 he went to California where he met and married Helen Waite, who had been born in Stockton, California, and studied at Berkeley. The Papashvilys came to Bucks County, Pennsylvania, in 1935 and established Ertoba Farm, the home in which they still live. George became an American citizen in 1944, and in 1945 he and Helen wrote *Anything Can Happen*, an account of his first years in America. It was an enormous success and still delights readers here and abroad. It has been translated into fifteen foreign languages, including Chinese, Japanese, and Urdu.

In his studio at Ertoba Farm, George carves his wonderful stone sculptures that have been shown in galleries and museums all over the country. He and Helen have written several other books, among them *Thanks to Noah* and *Yes and No Stories*, a collection of Georgian folk tales; Helen is the author of *All the Happy Endings*.